POWER EATING

SUSAN M. KLEINER, PhD, RD

High Performance Nutrition
Mercer Island, Washington

with
Maggie Greenwood-Robinson

Human Kinetics

Library of Congress Cataloging-in-Publication Data

Kleiner, Susan M.

   Power eating / Susan M. Kleiner, with Maggie Greenwood-Robinson.
     p. cm.
   Includes bibliographical references and index.
   ISBN 0-88011-702-8
   1. Athletes--Nutrition.   2. Bodybuilders--Nutrition.
  I. Greenwood-Robinson, Maggie.   II. Title.
  TX361.A8K595   1998   97-43566
  613.2'024796--dc21   CIP

ISBN: 0-88011-702-8

Copyright © 1998 by Human Kinetics Publishers, Inc.

Acquisitions Editor: Martin Barnard; **Developmental Editor:** Laura Casey Mast; **Assistant Editor:** Cynthia McEntire; **Editorial Assistants:** Laura Ward Majersky, Jennifer Simmons, Laura Seversen; **Copyeditor:** Judy Peterson; **Proofreader:** Myla Smith; **Indexer:** Gerry Lynn Messner; **Graphic Designer:** Nancy Rasmus; **Graphic Artist:** Yvonne Winsor; **Photo Editor:** Boyd LaFoon; **Cover Designer:** Jack Davis; **Photographer (interior):** Human Kinetics/Tom Roberts; **Illustrator:** M.R. Greenberg; **Printer:** Versa Press

Human Kinetics books are available at special discounts for bulk purchase. Special editions or book excerpts can also be created to specification. For details, contact the Special Sales Manager at Human Kinetics.

Printed in the United States of America   10 9 8 7 6 5 4 3 2 1

Human Kinetics
Web site: http://www.humankinetics.com/

United States: Human Kinetics
P.O. Box 5076
Champaign, IL 61825-5076
1-800-747-4457
e-mail: humank@hkusa.com

Canada: Human Kinetics, Box 24040
Windsor, ON N8Y 4Y9
1-800-465-7301 (in Canada only)
e-mail: humank@hkcanada.com

Europe: Human Kinetics, P.O. Box IW14
Leeds LS16 6TR, United Kingdom
(44) 1132 781708
e-mail: humank@hkeurope.com

Australia: Human Kinetics
57A Price Avenue
Lower Mitcham, South Australia 5062
(088) 277 1555
e-mail: humank@hkaustralia.com

New Zealand: Human Kinetics
P.O. Box 105-231, Auckland 1
(09) 523 3462
e-mail: humank@hknewz.com

CONTENTS

PREFACE

Power Eating is the book that I have always wanted to write. Since 1982, when I began researching strength training and began a personal strength-training program, I knew that this book needed to be written. But not until now has there been enough scientific information on the topic of nutrition, bodybuilding, and strength training to write a credible book. If you want to strength train to compete, stay healthy, or look great, you need this book. There is nothing else like it.

These are exciting times for strength trainers. Great discoveries are happening. We are beginning to understand what nutrients the body needs to support strength training and muscle building. There are finally supplements that really work. But deciphering the scientific information and separating fact from Madison Avenue promotional hype can be difficult.

This book contains 15 years of my professional experience working in the field of nutrition and strength training. From research with professional bodybuilders to practice with professional football players, I have honed a diet for strength training that will meet your individual needs.

Power Eating will teach you what you can't learn anywhere else. What are the body's basic nutritional requirements? Do you need to add any extra nutrients for strength training? Do supplements really work? What about fake sugars and fake fats? What harm can drugs do? Can you be a vegetarian and still build muscle? Can you cut weight safely and stay healthy? Are there any dietary tricks that will help you bulk up? What should you eat on competition day?

When it comes to designing your personal diet plan, I will do the work for you. Just pattern your plan after the eight diet plans that I have designed, and you'll achieve your goals.

My goal is to get your body where you want it to be, and keep you healthy, safe, and legal. With *Power Eating* you can do it all.

ACKNOWLEDGMENTS

My greatest appreciation goes to our editor, Martin Barnard, and my coauthor, Maggie Greenwood-Robinson, the visionary people who knew that this book's time had finally come, and could help me make it so. Many thanks to James Park for your excellent job of researching the details. Most importantly, thank you to my family for your love and support.

To Mom

FUELING UP FOR STRENGTH TRAINING

Think about how you would like to look and feel. Imagine yourself with a body that's fit and firm, with just the right amount of muscle. Imagine the joy of having high strength and energy that give you the power to perform, day in and day out.

Keep those images in your mind's eye. This book will show you how to achieve those goals by taking a few nips and tucks in one of the most important fitness factors of all—nutrition. But not just any type of nutrition. This is a book for people who strength train. And strength trainers have very specific nutritional needs that depend on the type and level of their activity.

What kind of strength trainer are you? Are you a bodybuilder, powerlifter, Olympic lifter, an athlete who strength trains for conditioning, or someone who works out with weights to stay in shape? Granted, these activities all have differing physical demands and differing nutritional requirements. That's why you will find several individualized strength-training diets in chapter 11. But the common denominator underlying the workouts of all strength-training athletes, from competitors to recreational exercisers, is their interest in the same thing: building lean muscle.

WHAT BUILDS MUSCLE?

Most certainly, strength training builds muscle. But for this construction to take place, you have to supply the construction material— namely, protein, carbohydrates, and fat. In a process called metabolism, the body breaks down these nutrients and uses the products to generate the energy required for growth and life.

During metabolism, proteins are broken down into amino acids. Cells use amino acids to make new proteins based on instructions supplied by DNA, our genetic management system. The DNA provides specific information on how amino acids are to be lined up and strung together. Once these instructions have been carried out, the cell has synthesized a new protein.

Based on this process, logic would tell you that the more protein you eat, the more muscle your body can construct. But it doesn't work that way. Excess protein is converted to carbohydrate to be used for energy, or to fat for storage.

The way to make muscles grow is not by gorging on protein but by demanding more from it—that is, by making it work harder. The muscles will respond by taking up the nutrients they need, including amino acids from protein metabolism, so that they can grow. If you work your muscles hard, muscle cells will synthesize the protein the muscles need.

WHAT FUELS MUSCLES?

To work your muscles hard, you have to provide the right kind of muscle fuel. Muscle cells, like all cells, run on a high-energy compound known as adenosine triphosphate (ATP). One of the energy molecules, ATP makes muscles contract, conducts nerve impulses, and promotes other cellular energy processes. Muscle cells make ATP by combining oxygen with nutrients from food, mainly carbohydrate. Fat is also used for fuel by muscles, but fat can be broken down only when oxygen is present. Muscle cells really prefer to burn carbohydrate, store fat, and use protein for growth and repair.

Your cells generate ATP through any one of three energy systems: the phosphagen system, the glycolytic system, and the oxidative system.

The phosphagen system rebuilds ATP by supplying a compound called creatine phosphate (CP). Once ATP is used up, it must be replenished from additional food and oxygen. During short intense bursts of exercise like weight training or sprinting, available oxygen is exhausted by the working muscles. At that point, CP kicks in to supply energy for a few short seconds of work. CP can help create ATP when ATP is depleted.

Any intense exercise lasting for 3 to 15 seconds will rapidly deplete ATP and CP in a muscle; they must then be replaced. Replenishing ATP and CP is the job of the other energy systems in the body.

The glycolytic system makes glucose available to the muscles, either from the breakdown of dietary carbohydrates during digestion or from the breakdown of muscle and liver glycogen, the stored form of carbohydrate. In a process called glycolysis, glycogen is disassembled into glucose in the muscles and, through a series of chemical reactions, ultimately converted to more ATP.

The glycogen reserve in your muscles can supply enough energy for about two to three minutes of short-burst exercise at a time. If sufficient oxygen is available to the muscle cell, a lot of ATP will be made from glucose. If oxygen is absent or in short supply, then the muscles produce a waste product from glucose called lactic acid. A buildup of lactic acid in a working muscle creates a burning sensation, and causes the muscle to fatigue and stop contracting. Lactic acid exits the muscle when oxygen is available to replenish CP and ATP. A brief rest period gives the body time to deliver oxygen to the muscles, and you can continue exercising.

The third energy system in your body is the oxidative system. This system helps fuel aerobic exercise and other endurance activities. Although the oxidative system can handle the energy needs of endurance exercise, all three energy systems kick in to some degree during endurance exercise. The phosphagen and glycolytic energy systems dominate when you are strength training.

Oxygen is not a direct source of energy for exercise; it is used as an ingredient to produce large amounts of ATP from other energy sources. The oxidative system works as follows: You breathe in oxygen, which is subsequently taken up from your lungs by the blood. Your heart pumps oxygen-rich blood to tissues, including muscle. Hemoglobin, an iron-containing protein of the blood, carries oxygen to the cells to enable them to produce energy. Myoglobin, another type of iron-containing protein, carries oxygen primarily to muscle cells. Inside muscle cells, carbohydrates and fats are converted into energy through a series of energy-producing reactions.

Your body's ability to produce energy via any one of these three systems can be improved with the right training diet and exercise program. The result is a fat-burning, muscle-building metabolism.

NUTRITION PRINCIPLES FOR STRENGTH TRAINERS

If you are serious about improving your physique and your strength-training performance, you'll do everything you can to achieve success. Unfortunately, advice given to strength trainers today is a hodgepodge of fact and fantasy. What I'd like to do is separate one from the other by sharing several basic principles with you—principles that all strength trainers can follow to get in shape and achieve their personal best in performance. These principles are the same ones I have advocated for world-class athletes, Olympic contenders, and recreational strength trainers for more than 15 years. Let's review them here.

1. Vary Your Diet

You have probably admired the physiques of bodybuilders in magazines. And for good reason. They are muscular, well defined, and in near-perfect proportion. The picture of health, right? Wrong—in many cases. The first study I ever conducted investigated the training diets of male competitive bodybuilders. What I found was that they ate a lot of calories, roughly 6,000 calories a day or more. The worrisome finding about this study was that they ate, on average, more than 200 grams of fat a day. That's almost as much fat as you'd find in two sticks of butter! Short-term, that's enough to make most people sick. Eaten habitually over time, such an enormous amount of fat will lead to heart disease.

Bodybuilding diets, especially pre-contest diets, tend to be very monotonous, with the same foods showing up on the plate day after day. The worst example I've ever seen was a bodybuilder who ate chicken, pepper, vinegar, and rice for three days straight while preparing for competition. The problem with such a diet is that it lacks variety, and without a variety of foods, you miss out on loads of nutrients essential for peak health.

Bodybuilders, on average, don't eat much in the way of fruit, dairy products, and red meat. Fruit, of course, is packed with disease-fighting, health-building antioxidants and phytochemicals. Dairy products supply important nutrients like bone-building calcium. And red meat is an important source of vital minerals like iron and zinc.

When such foods are limited or eliminated, potentially serious deficiencies begin to show up. In studies I've done, and in studies others have done, the most common deficiencies observed are those of calcium and zinc, particularly during the pre-competition season. In fact, many female bodybuilders have dangerous shortages of these minerals, and they may have the shortages year round. A chronic short supply of calcium increases the risk of osteoporosis, a crippling bone-thinning disease. Although a woman's need for zinc is small (15 milligrams a day), adequate zinc is an impenetrable line of defense when it comes to protecting women from disease and infection. In short, deficits of these minerals can harm health and performance. But the good news is that some skim milk, red meat, and dark meat poultry added back into the diet will help alleviate some of these problems. A three-ounce portion of lean sirloin beef has about six milligrams of zinc; nonfat, 1, or 2 percent milk has about one milligram of zinc in one eight-ounce glass; and three ounces of dark meat turkey have about four milligrams of zinc.

Another nutritional problem among bodybuilders is fluid restriction. Just before a contest, bodybuilders don't drink much water, fearing it will inflate their physiques to the point of blurring their muscular definition. Compounding the problem, many bodybuilders take diuretics and laxatives, a practice that flushes more water, plus precious minerals called electrolytes, from the body. Generally, bodybuilders compete in a dehydrated state. In one contest, I saw two people pass out on stage—one because of severe dehydration, the other because of an electrolyte imbalance.

After a competition, bodybuilders tend to go hog wild. There's nothing wrong with this, as long as it's a temporary splurge. But such dietary indulgence over a long time can lead to extra fat pounds you surely don't want.

Bodybuilders, however, do a lot of things right, especially during the training season. They eat several meals throughout the day—a practice that nutritionists recommend to the general public.

2. Follow a High-Carbohydrate Diet

It is well known, too, that most athletes, strength trainers included, don't eat enough carbohydrates, the primary fuel food. Most athletes eat diets in which only half of their total daily calories come from carbs, when 70 percent of their daily calories should be consumed as carbs. Lots of bodybuilders practice low-carbohydrate dieting because they believe it promotes faster weight loss. The problem with these diets is that they deplete glycogen, the body's storage form of carbohydrate. Once available glycogen stores are emptied, the body starts burning protein from tissues (including muscle tissue) to meet its demand for energy. You lose hard-earned muscle as a result.

Bodybuilders and other strength trainers shy away from carbs, particularly breads and pastas. They think these foods will make them fat—a food myth that is partially responsible for the lopsided proportions of carbohydrate, fat, and protein in strength-training diets, which are typically too high in protein.

Carbs are probably the most important nutrient for losing fat and building muscle. By the time you finish this book, you'll be convinced of this truth!

3. Consume Enough Calories

A key to feeling energized is to eat the right amount of calories to power your body for hard training. A lack of calories will definitely make you feel like a wet dishrag by the end of your workout.

A diet that provides less than 1,600 calories per day generally does not contain all the vitamins and minerals you need to stay healthy, prevent disease, and perform well. Very low-calorie diets followed for longer than two weeks can be hazardous to your health. Nor do they provide the Recommended Dietary Allowances (RDA) of enough of the nutrients needed for good health.

Historically, the RDA is the national standard for the amount of carbohydrate, protein, fat, vitamins, and minerals we need in our diets to avoid deficiency diseases and maintain growth and health. But under certain conditions—stress, illness, malnutrition, and exercise— we may require a much higher intake of certain nutrients. Studies have shown that athletes in particular may have to exceed the RDA of many nutrients. Some competitive bodybuilders have estimated their caloric intake to be greater than 6,000 calories a day during the off-season—roughly three times the RDA for the average person (2,000 calories a day for a woman and 2,700 calories a day for a man).

How much you need of each nutrient depends on a number of factors, including your age and sex, how hard you train, and whether you are a competitive or recreational strength trainer, among other considerations. Generally, we find that strength trainers need to eat more carbohydrates and may be wise to supplement with antioxidants and certain minerals. You'll learn more about these issues as you read this book. If you are trying to gain muscle and lose body fat, eating enough calories and taking in enough nutrients will make the difference between success and failure.

4. Stop Megadosing

A writer in a popular bodybuilding magazine once wrote: "Body-builders seem to believe that nothing succeeds like excess. That if something is good for you, twice as much is even better. That too much is never enough."

In many ways, this statement prevails as a motto in strength-training nutrition, particularly when it comes to protein and supplements. Thus, strength trainers and bodybuilders tend to megadose

POWER PROFILES

Calories are certainly important in building muscle mass; however, the source of those calories is key if you want to maximize muscle and minimize body fat. Case in point: a professional rookie football player who wanted to lose weight to improve his speed on the field. Unless he trimmed down, his chance to be on the team was in jeopardy, so he needed a dramatic nutritional rescue.

This football player was eating slightly more than 7,000 calories a day. Broken down, those calories figured out to 17 percent protein, 32 percent fat, and about 49 percent carbohydrate. In daily fat grams, he was consuming a whopping 250 grams a day. The composition of his calories was an impediment to losing fat. I reconfigured his diet to 5,680 calories a day, with 12.5 percent of those calories coming from protein, 25 percent from fat, and 62.5 percent from carbs. That mix would slash his fat grams to a healthier 142 grams a day.

He was eating a lot of hidden fat in foods like fried chicken, whole milk, and fast foods. For the high-fat foods, we substituted skinless chicken breasts, 1 percent milk, and fast-food choices such as salads and frozen yogurt that were lower in fat. Additionally, we modified some of his favorite dishes such as sweet potato pie into lower fat versions. He also began to load up on complex carbs like rice, pasta, bread, and vegetables. Plus, he cut his meat allotment down to about eight ounces a day.

The upshot of these dietary changes was that he lost the weight, made the team, and had a great season. He is still a professional football player.

on supplements and foods, thinking that the more they take or eat, the more muscle they'll build. Nothing could be further from the truth. You require a specific amount of nutrients for muscle building, based on your individual needs. Eat more food than you need and it turns to unsightly fat. And if you megadose on supplements, the surplus is excreted, or can be toxic to your body.

Protein, Strength, and Muscle Building

For generations, athletes have believed that a high-protein diet will increase strength. This myth can be historically traced to a famous Greek athlete, Milo of Crotona, in the sixth century B.C. One of the strongest men in Greece, Milo was the wrestling victor in five Olympic Games and in many of the other sacred festivals. As the legend goes, he applied progressive resistance training by lifting a growing calf daily, and when the calf was four years old, he carried it the length of the Olympian stadium, killed, roasted, and ate it. It is written that his normal daily intake of meat was about 20 pounds.

In the sixties and seventies, protein was thought to be a miracle food because muscle magazines hyped it so much. Thus, bodybuilders and other athletes would follow diets made up mostly of meat, milk, and eggs. The raw egg milkshake was particularly popular, thanks to Rocky Balboa. Why would anyone want to swill such a concoction? Answer: misinformation. Articles and advertising from those days continue to falsely communicate the notion that the protein from raw foods, and eggs in particular, is more available to our bodies for building muscle, compared to cooked foods.

Not only is this notion absolutely untrue, it is dangerous to believe. A protein molecule is a string of amino acids connected together like a strand of pearls. If two strands of pearls were wound together, and then twisted to double up on each other, they would resemble a protein molecule.

Heating or cooking the protein molecule unwinds the string of amino acids, straightens it out, and finally separates it into smaller pieces. This is the process of heat denaturing, which is similar to the process of chemical denaturing, otherwise known as digestion. Cooking food protein can begin the digestive process, and can actually decrease the net energy that the body must expend during digestion.

Eating raw eggs is a hazardous practice because eggs may be contaminated with the microorganisms that cause salmonella poisoning. Cooking eggs destroys bacteria, eliminating the risk of contracting this serious food-borne illness. Clearly, the idea of eating raw eggs to build muscle size and strength is a food myth. Raw eggs should be avoided completely.

Today, amino acid supplements—a modern twist on the high-protein myth—are promoted to increase lean body mass and improve muscular performance.

Sport nutrition research has debunked all these protein myths. We now know that the most important dietary factor influencing muscle growth and strength is a carb-rich diet. Strength-training athletes do need more protein than the general population, but it's not as much as you may think. In my many years of working with strength trainers, I've never seen anyone who was protein deficient, not even a vegetarian!

The Scoop on Supplements

Since 1972, sales of dietary supplements have increased sixfold, from $500 million to $3 billion. Forty-five percent of all men and 55 percent of women take dietary supplements. Those of us who regularly use nutrient supplements spend an average of $32 a year on vitamin and mineral pills.

That means that a lot of us are spending much more than the average, because these statistics only cover what we call essential nutrient supplements—the commonly recognized vitamins and minerals we must consume in our diets to stay healthy and avoid deficiencies. Typically, the only disease a vitamin or mineral will cure is one caused by a deficiency of that vitamin or mineral. It is preferable to consume these nutrients as food. But when you don't eat enough in your diet, supplementation with a daily multiple vitamin and mineral pill may be a very important way to get what you need.

Nonessential supplements are chemicals or compounds that don't cause classical signs of deficiency diseases if they are absent from the diet. Put another way, these supplements aren't required to maintain health or boost performance. We can certainly perform without nonessential supplements like MCT oil or chromium picolinate, but many strength trainers wouldn't be without them. Could we reach new levels of performance if we included some nonessential supplements in our diets?

It's hard to say for sure, although the links between diet and performance are becoming clearer all the time. We have also come to realize that these links are more complex than we thought. Every day we read about new research discoveries relating to some factor in food that promises to boost energy or prevent disease. Sometimes these discoveries tell us that some factor previously considered nonessential may be very important in helping improve health and energy.

Such information is all that supplement manufacturers need to hear. Once one small piece of evidence surfaces—even in a single rat study—that a certain food factor may be helpful in preventing disease, building muscle, or enhancing performance, the next place you see that factor is in a supplement.

Unfortunately, supplement manufacturers don't have to follow the same rigorous review process that is required for new drugs.

Supplements are legally considered food, not drugs. The United States Food and Drug Administration (FDA) expects the same kind of truth in labeling with supplements as it does with food. But in contrast to drugs, supplements do not have to be proven to work before they are placed on the market.

Unless someone gets sick from taking a supplement and reports it to the FDA, supplement manufacturers rarely have to prove their claims. So consumer beware. There may be no truth, part truth, or full truth to the claims for the use of a supplement. Before you believe everything that you read on a supplement label or advertisement, try to get some facts.

WHERE DO YOU STAND NOW?

Analyze your present diet now to see exactly what you're eating, particularly in terms of the three energy nutrients. You should also analyze how much water you're drinking, since water is a critical nutrient. This analysis will make the following chapters more relevant and interesting to you. For example, when you're reading about protein, you may wonder how much protein you're eating now. With this analysis handy, you can find out quickly.

Using the chart provided, record everything you eat over the course of three days. Choose days that best represent your typical diet. Be as accurate as you can in terms of the amount of food you eat. Use a food composition guide, either in book or software format, to help you figure out nutrients and calories. Table 1.1 (page 12) is a simple form you can use to record your food and analyze your diet.

Sport Nutrition Fact vs. Fiction: Are Carbs Fattening?

Researchers investigating diet, weight loss, chronic disease, and diet and exercise, have debunked the myth that breads and starchy foods (high-carbohydrate foods) are fattening and should be avoided. On the contrary, starchy foods are low in calories, and the most healthful diet for weight loss, disease prevention, and physical performance is a high-carbohydrate diet.

The problem with eating high-carb foods like breads, noodles, and potatoes is not the foods themselves, but what we put on them. The

TABLE 1.1	Three-Day Food Record					
Food	Amount	Protein (g)	Carbs (g)	Fat (g)	Calories

Day 1

Totals

Day 2

Totals

Day 3

myth that starchy foods are fattening should be changed to the truism that the butter, spreads, creams, and sauces on starchy foods are fattening. High-fat foods are high-calorie foods. By replacing regular butter, spreads, and sour creams with their new low-fat and nonfat versions, we can eliminate most of the high-fat, high-calorie fare that often accompanies these low-fat, low-calorie, high-carbohydrate foods.

Sport Nutrition Fact vs. Fiction: Organic Foods—Are They Better for You?

With the amount of food strength trainers eat, many are opting to go organic to avoid the chemical fertilizers, pesticides, and additives used in many foods. Do you get an advantage in buying organic foods?

In general, organically grown foods are grown in soil enriched with organic fertilizers, rather than synthetic fertilizers, and treated only with nonsynthetic pesticides. Organic farms use a soil-building program that promotes vibrant soil and healthy plants, usually including crop rotations and biological pest control. Presently, the job of regulating the organic farming industry is left up to the states. The states vary in their enforcement of regulations and their oversight of organic farming, and not all states have instituted organic programs or statutory definitions. In 1990, Congress passed a law defining a federal standard for organic farming methods. The bill has not been implemented yet, but it was slated to be in place by 1997.

Advocates of organic foods claim that they are more nutritious, and present fewer of the health hazards associated with pesticide contamination. In general, this argument does not seem to hold up. Some surveys find similar pesticide levels in both organically and conventionally grown foods. Even when organic foods are grown according to certification standards, contaminated run-off water, contaminated shifting soil, and airborne pesticides may still result in pesticides being present on food.

Organically grown food does not have greater nutritive value than food grown with conventional methods. The soil nutrients from natural fertilizers are no different from the nutrients in chemical fertilizers made in factories. The genetic makeup of the food will also determine that particular food's nutrient content and needs.

The freshness of organic foods may also be questionable. In many states, an efficient production, distribution, and retail sales system is not in place for organic produce, and the slow movement of the produce from field to market may permit wilting and nutrient losses.

Organically grown produce costs much more than its conventionally grown counterpart. Depending on supply and demand, this difference can be quite significant.

According to Miles McEvoy, program manager for the Washington State Department of Agriculture Organic Food Program, organic foods are not safer and they are not better. His reason for promoting organic farming is that it is "a more environmentally benign way of producing food."

Organic farming methods are less harmful to the environment than conventional methods. The use of natural products helps to improve the soil. Organic pest control generally relies on preventive measures such as crop rotation and biological controls. These methods place little to no stress on the earth or its wildlife inhabitants.

In the end, the choice is yours. Purchasing organic foods is not just a nutritional issue, but a political and social issue as well. Nutritionally speaking, it's clearly important to eat a variety of foods to ensure a balanced nutrient intake, and to lessen pesticide contamination from any one source. Despite the use of pesticides, populations that eat large amounts of fruits and vegetables have lower rates of cancer than populations eating few fruits and vegetables.

You'll pay more for organic produce, so if your pocketbook is light, buy fresh conventional produce and follow these guidelines for reducing pesticide residues in foods:

- Wash fresh produce in water. Use a scrub brush, and rinse the foods thoroughly under running water.
- Use a knife to peel an orange or grapefruit; do not bite into the peel.
- Discard the outer leaves of leafy vegetables such as cabbage and lettuce.
- Peel waxed fruit and vegetables; waxes don't wash off and can seal in pesticide residues.
- Peel vegetables such as carrots and fruits such as apples when appropriate. (Peeling removes pesticides that remain in or on the peel, but also removes fibers, vitamins, and minerals.)

Chapter 2

PROTEIN: THE KEY TO MANUFACTURING MUSCLE

Inside your body a marvelous process of self-repair takes place, day in and day out, and it all has to do with protein, the nutrient responsible for building and maintaining body tissues.

Proteins are present everywhere in the body—in muscle, bones, connective tissue, blood vessels, blood cells, skin, hair, and fingernails. These proteins are constantly being lost or broken down due to normal, physiological wear and tear, and must be replaced. For example, about one-half of the total amount of protein in muscle tissue is broken down and replaced every 150 days.

The mechanism by which this occurs is really quite amazing. During digestion, protein in food is dismantled by other proteins (enzymes) into subunits called amino acids. In this form, amino acids can enter cells, where other enzymes, acting on instructions from DNA, put them back together as the new proteins needed to build and repair tissue. No other system in the world repairs itself so wonderfully. Every day, this process goes on and life continues.

Under any condition of growth—childhood, pregnancy, muscle building—the body manufactures more cells than are lost. From an energy source such as carbohydrate or fat, the body can manufacture many of the materials needed to make new cells. But to replace and build new proteins, it must have protein from food. Unlike carbohydrates and fat, protein contains nitrogen, and nitrogen is required to synthesize new proteins.

Protein, therefore, is absolutely necessary for the maintenance, replacement, and growth of body tissue. But protein has other uses, too. The body uses protein to make the hormones that regulate your metabolism, maintain the body's water balance, protect against disease, transport nutrients in and out of cells, carry oxygen, and regulate blood clotting.

PROTEIN AND MUSCLE BUILDING

Protein is a key player in the repair and construction of muscle tissue following exercise. By lifting weights, you force your muscles to lengthen when they want to contract. This action causes microscopic tears in your muscle fibers (the reason for the muscle soreness you feel a day or two after your workout). In response, your body makes muscle fibers bigger and stronger to protect against future insults.

The construction material for this process comes primarily from dietary protein, which is broken down in digestion into amino acids. As previously explained, amino acids enter the bloodstream and are transported to cells to be synthesized into body proteins. Your muscle cells use amino acids to create more muscle protein. There are two major types of muscle protein, actin and myosin. During muscular contraction, these muscle proteins slide over each other like two pieces of a telescope. When you build muscle, you're basically increasing the amount of actin and myosin in your muscles. This makes the muscle fibers increase in diameter, get stronger, and contract more powerfully.

PROTEIN AND STRENGTH-TRAINING PERFORMANCE

It would seem that the more construction material (protein) you supply your body, the more muscle you would build. At least that's the train of thought strength athletes have followed for ages. But it doesn't quite work that way. In other words, eating twice as much protein won't make your muscles twice as big. Furthermore, one problem with eating too much protein is that the excess can be stored as body fat.

To build muscle, you must be in a positive nitrogen balance. Nitrogen leaves the body primarily in the urine. Nitrogen lost by excretion must be replaced by nitrogen taken in from food. Protein contains a fairly large concentration of nitrogen. Generally, healthy adults are in a nitrogen equilibrium, or zero balance—that is, their protein intake meets their protein requirement. A positive nitrogen balance means that the body is retaining dietary protein and using it to synthesize new tissue. If more nitrogen is excreted than was consumed, the nitrogen balance is negative. The body has lost nitrogen—and therefore protein. A negative nitrogen balance over time is dangerous, leading to muscle wasting and disease.

Achieving a positive nitrogen balance doesn't necessarily mean you have to eat more protein. Muscle cells take up the exact amount of nutrients (including amino acids from dietary protein) they need for growth. And strength training helps them better utilize the protein that's available.

This fact was clearly demonstrated in 1995 by a group of Tufts University researchers led by Wayne W. Campbell. The researchers took a group of older men and women (ages 56 to 80) who had never lifted weights before, placed them on either a low-protein diet or a high-protein diet, and measured their nitrogen balance before and after participation in a 12 week strength-training program. The low-protein diet was actually based on the RDA for protein (0.8 grams per kilogram of body weight daily). The high-protein diet was twice the RDA (1.6 grams per kilogram of body weight daily). The researchers wanted to see what effects each diet had on nitrogen balance during strength training.

What they found out was interesting. Strength training enhanced nitrogen retention in both groups—in other words, protein was being retained and used to synthesize new tissue. However, in the low-protein group, there was even better utilization of protein. Strength training caused the body to adapt and meet the demand for protein—even when the bare minimum requirement for protein was eaten each day. This shows how marvelously the body adjusts to what is available, and how strength training makes muscle cells more efficient at using available protein to synthesize new tissue.

So exactly how much protein should you eat for maximum performance and results? That is a question that has been hotly debated in science for more than 100 years, and by athletes since the time of the ancient Greeks. There are several reasons why it has been difficult for nutrition scientists to reach a consensus on protein intake. One has to do with the type of exercise you do, and how frequently you do it. In endurance exercise, for example, protein can act as kind of a spare fuel tank, kicking in amino acids to supply fuel. If protein is in short supply, the endurance athlete can peter out easily. In strength sports, additional dietary protein is needed to provide enough amino acids to synthesize protein in the muscles.

For generations, strength trainers have looked to protein as the nutritional panacea for muscle building. Is there any scientific basis to this belief? Possibly. Some exploding new research proves that as a strength trainer, you may benefit from eating some extra protein.

Strength training helps reverse the effects of aging.

Here's the latest word from science on the subject, as described by Peter Lemon, November 11–12, 1994, at the Nutritional Ergogenic Aids Conference sponsored by the Gatorade Sports Institute.

Protein Benefits Older Strength Trainers

It's no secret that as you age, you can lose muscle mass, strength, and function, partly due to inactivity. One way to reverse the downhill slide is by strength training. Study after study has shown that you can make significant muscle gains well up into your 90s if you strength train.

Now scientific research indicates that senior strength trainers can get a real boost from additional protein. At Tufts University, researchers gave supplemental protein to a group of elderly strength trainers, while a control group took no supplements. The result? Based on CAT scans of muscle, the supplement group gained much more muscle mass than the control group did.

Protein Benefits Younger Strength Trainers, Too

But what if you're not yet in your golden years? Can you get the same benefits from extra protein? One study says yes. Two groups of young bodybuilders following a four-week strength-training program followed the same diet, but with one exception. One group ate 2.3 grams of protein per kilogram of body weight (a very large amount), compared to 1.3 grams of protein per kilogram of body weight in the other group. By the end of the study, both groups had gained muscle. But those eating the higher amount of protein had gained five times more muscle!

How High Can You Go?

At Kent State University, researchers divided strength trainers into three groups: (1) a low-protein group on a diet of 0.9 grams of protein per kilogram of body weight, which approximates the protein recommendation for sedentary people; (2) a group eating 1.4 grams of protein per kilogram of body weight; and (3) a group eating 2.4 grams of protein per kilogram of body weight. There were also control groups, both sedentary subjects and strength-training subjects.

Two exciting findings emerged. First, increasing protein intake to 1.4 grams triggered protein synthesis (an indicator of muscle growth) in strength trainers. There were no such changes in the low-protein group. Second, upping protein intake from 1.4 grams to 2.4 grams produced no further protein synthesis. This latter finding suggested that a plateau had been reached, meaning that the subjects got more protein than they could use at 2.4 grams.

The research appears to indicate that if you strength train and eat more protein, you are going to enhance muscle development and preservation. But does this mean you should start piling protein on your plate? Not necessarily. Studies should always be interpreted with caution. Let's talk about how much protein you really need for your individual activity level.

Your Individual Requirements

As a strength trainer or bodybuilder, you do need more protein than a less active person. In fact, your requirement is higher than the current RDA of 0.8 grams of protein per kilogram of body weight a day, which is based on the needs of nonexercisers. But it's only slightly higher. (Don't forget; your body can work with a protein intake that meets the RDA.) Plus, individual protein requirements vary, based on whether you're in a muscle-building phase, doing aerobic exercise on a regular basis, or dieting for competition. Here's a closer look.

For Muscle Building

With increases in training intensity, you need additional protein to support muscle growth and increases in certain blood compounds. Based on the latest research with strength trainers, I recommend that you eat 1.6 grams of protein per kilogram of body weight a day. Here's how you would figure that requirement if you weigh 150 pounds or 68 kilograms (a kilogram equals 2.2 pounds):

$$1.6 \text{ g of protein per kg of body weight} \times 68 \text{ kg} = 109 \text{ g of protein a day}$$

Are you a brand new strength trainer? If so, you may need to eat more protein than a veteran strength trainer typically consumes—as much as 40 percent more. Vegetarian strength trainers who eat no animal products should take in 2.0 grams of protein per kilogram of body weight a day to make sure their diets are providing all the amino acids their bodies require.

If You're Doing Aerobic Exercise, Too

On average, most strength trainers and bodybuilders perform an hour or two of intense weight training daily, plus five or more hours a week of aerobic exercise. If you are in this category, your protein needs are further elevated. Here's why.

During aerobic exercise lasting 60 to 90 minutes, certain amino acids—the so-called branched-chain amino acids—are used for energy in small amounts, particularly when the body is running low on carbohydrates, its preferred fuel source. One of the branched-chain amino acids, leucine, is broken down to make another amino acid called alanine, which is converted by the liver into blood sugar (glucose) for energy. This glucose is transported to the working muscles to be used for energy. The harder you work out aerobically, the more leucine your body breaks down for extra fuel.

Given this special use of amino acids as an energy source, you should increase your protein intake if your training program includes aerobics. You may require as much as 1.8 grams of protein per kilogram of body weight. Using the above example, you would calculate your requirements as follows:

1.8 g of protein per kg of body weight × 68 kg = 123 g of protein a day

When Dieting for Competition

When cutting calories to lean out for competition, you risk losing muscle mass, along with body fat. Because muscle is the body's most metabolically active tissue, losing it compromises the ability of your body to burn fat. What's more, no bodybuilder wants to lose muscle prior to competition. One way to prevent diet-related muscle loss is to consume adequate protein while you're preparing for competition. Dieting bodybuilders need between 1.8 and 2.0 grams of protein per kilogram of body weight a day. For example:

2.0 g of protein per kg of body weight × 68 kg = 136 g of protein a day

For more information on getting cut for competition, see chapter 9.

BEWARE OF HIGH-PROTEIN DIETS

High-protein diets promising quick weight loss continue to be the rage. These diets let you fill up on beef, chicken, fish, and eggs, with little emphasis on other foods like vegetables and grains.

What's wrong with such a diet? To begin with, high-protein diets are high in fat. The protein in animal foods is often coupled with large amounts of saturated fat and cholesterol. Excess dietary fat can make you gain body fat and is damaging to your heart.

High-protein diets are often low in fiber, too. Without enough bulk to move things along, your whole digestive system slows down to a crawl. That can lead to constipation, diverticulosis, and other intestinal disorders.

Adding insult to injury, high-protein diets can also flush too much calcium from the body. High protein diets cause an increase in calcium loss in the urine. Over a lifetime, this loss can be unhealthy, particularly for women who need adequate levels of calcium to protect against the bone-thinning disease osteoporosis.

There's more: excess dietary protein is rough on the kidneys. The kidneys process the nitrogen wastes generated by protein metabolism. A system overloaded with protein interferes with the kidney's ability to properly eliminate these wastes, possibly setting the stage for kidney disease.

High-protein diets are also dehydrating. Within the first week on a high-protein diet, you can lose a lot of weight, depending on your initial weight and body fat percentage. You get on the scale, see an exhilarating weight loss, and feel wonderful. But most of this loss is water. You could be very dehydrated as a result. That spells trouble. A mere three-pound water weight loss in a 150 pound person can make you feel draggy and thus hurt your exercise performance. The minute you go off this diet and eat some carbohydrates, water surges back into your tissues and you regain the lost water weight.

Clearly, your focus should not be on protein, but on a balance of nutrients. In fact, protein should comprise approximately 15 percent of your total daily calories. In chapter 10, you'll learn how to design your own personal eating plan, one that contains the right amount of protein, carbohydrates, and fat to help you build muscle and stay lean.

RED MEAT

Is red meat a good source of protein for strength trainers? Yes. But you may have shied away from red meat in the past because it tends to be very high in fat and dietary cholesterol. Red meat, however, is a good source of protein, as well as iron and zinc.

Iron is necessary for manufacturing hemoglobin, which carries oxygen from the lungs to the tissues, and myoglobin, another transporter of oxygen found only in muscle tissue. The iron in red meat and other animal proteins is known as heme iron. The body absorbs heme iron better than it absorbs iron from plant foods, known as nonheme iron.

Zinc is a busy mineral. As one of the most widely distributed minerals in the body, zinc helps the body absorb vitamins, especially the B-complex vitamins. It is also involved in digestion and metabolism and is essential for growth. Like iron, zinc from animal proteins is absorbed better than zinc from plant foods.

Red meat is a good source of protein, zinc, and iron.

Red meat clearly has some nutritional pluses. The key is to control the amount of fat you get from meat. Here's how to do that.

1.   Serving size. Keep the serving size moderate since about three ounces of lean beef contains just 8.4 grams of total fat. A three-ounce serving is about the size of a deck of cards or the palm of a woman's hand. To get three ounces of cooked meat, start with four ounces of uncooked, boneless meat.

2.   Cut of meat. Certain cuts of meat are leaner than most. Called the "skinniest six," top round, top loin, round tip, tenderloin, sirloin, and eye of round are the leanest cuts you can select. Each three-ounce cooked and trimmed serving contains under 8.6 grams of total fat, under 77 mg of dietary cholesterol, and under 180 calories.

Beef is also graded according to fat marbling: prime, choice, and select. Select is the leanest grade. When selecting beef, purchase lean cuts closely trimmed of fat, or trim them yourself at home before you cook.

Pork is also a leaner meat than it used to be. The leanest cuts of pork come from the loin and leg areas, and a three-ounce cooked and trimmed portion of any of these cuts contains less than nine grams of fat and less than 180 calories. Lamb and veal are also lower in fat content than beef. Follow the same guidelines for selecting lean cuts.

3.   Preparation. To keep a lean cut lean and tasty after cooking, it must be handled and prepared properly. Because leaner cuts have less fat in the meat to keep them moist and juicy, the method of preparing the meat is important. More tender cuts, like loin cuts, can be broiled or grilled and served immediately. Avoid overcooking.

Less tender cuts, like round cuts, should be marinated to tenderize. Because it is the acid in the marinade (vinegar, citrus juice, or wine) that tenderizes the meat, oil can be replaced with water without diminishing the tenderizing effect. To improve tenderness of roasts, carve into thin slices, on the diagonal, and across the grain when possible.

GOING MEATLESS, STAYING MUSCULAR

Can you be a vegetarian and still build muscle? Absolutely—as long as you plan your diet properly. The key is to mix and match foods so that you get the right balance of amino acids each day.

You can think of amino acids as a construction crew hired to build a house. Each crew member has a specific function, from framing to wiring. If just one crew member calls off, then the construction job doesn't get finished. It's the same with amino acids.

There are 20 amino acids, which are joined in various combinations to construct the proteins required for growth and tissue repair. For your body to build protein, all of these amino acids must be on the job. If just one amino acid is missing or found in a low amount, protein construction comes to a halt.

Of the 20 amino acids, nine cannot be made by the body; they must be supplied by the food you eat. These nine amino acids are called the essential amino acids. The other 11, which can be manufactured by the body, are known as the nonessential amino acids. Your body makes nonessential amino acids from carbohydrates and nitrogen and by chemically altering essential and nonessential amino acids. The essential and nonessential amino acids are listed in table 2.1.

Foods that contain all nine essential amino acids are called complete proteins. Proteins found in dairy products, eggs, meat, poultry, fish, and other animal sources are complete proteins. Various plant foods typically provide incomplete proteins that either lack or are low in a particular essential amino acid. The essential amino acid that is missing or in short supply is called the limiting amino acid.

To get enough essential amino acids from a vegetarian diet, select foods that complement each other's limiting amino acid. In other words, mix and match foods during the day so that food low in an essential amino acid is balanced by one that's higher in the same

POWER PROFILES

I once worked with a professional basketball player, who, for philosophical reasons, was a lacto-vegetarian. A lacto-vegetarian eats no animal foods except for eggs and dairy products. Very determined, he wanted to know how he could stick to his vegetarian game plan, both on the road and at home.

Unexpectedly, this player's biggest problem was not protein. He was getting plenty of protein from eating dairy products. But he wasn't getting enough iron, selenium, and zinc—minerals that are plentiful in flesh foods. Also, his diet was very high in fat, since he was eating a lot of cheese-laden vegetable lasagna.

To solve the mineral problem, he began taking a mineral supplement containing the RDA of the minerals he was lacking. After basketball practice, he started drinking one or two meal-replacement beverages, which contain extra nutrients and fit perfectly into a lacto-vegetarian diet.

With my help, he discovered several new low-fat recipes, like vegetarian chili, that could be packed for road trips and eaten for dinner as long as he had a microwave oven in his hotel room. He took dried fruit on the road, too. An eat-anywhere snack, dried fruit is loaded with energy-packed calories.

At home, he began to vary his diet using vegetarian staples such as beans, tofu, rice, and peanut butter. By varying his diet, he was also packing in plenty of quality calories to fuel both training and competition. Equally important, he learned he could be a strict lacto-vegetarian, in keeping with his beliefs, and do it successfully.

TABLE 2.1	Essential and Nonessential Amino Acids	
Essential		**Nonessential**
Histidine		Alanine
Isoleucine		Arginine
Leucine		Asparagine
Lysine		Aspartic acid
Methionine		Cysteine (cystine)
Phenylalanine		Glutamic acid
Threonine		Glutamine
Tryptophan		Glycine
Valine		Proline
		Serine
		Tyrosine

amino acid. For example, grains contain a limited amount of lysine but a higher amount of methionine. Legumes such as navy beans, kidney beans, or black beans are high in lysine but low in methionine. Thus, by combining grains and legumes, you create a complete protein meal. Soybeans are an exception and are considered a complete protein. Other fully nutritious protein combinations include the following:

- Rice and beans
- Corn and beans
- Corn and lima beans
- Corn tortillas and refried beans
- Pasta and bean soup
- Soybeans and seeds

If you are a vegetarian who chooses to eat milk and eggs, you needn't worry about combining complete protein foods. The protein in milk, eggs, cheeses, and other dairy products contains all the essential amino acids you need for tissue growth, repair, and maintenance. A word of caution, though: dairy products can be high in fat. So be sure to choose nonfat dairy foods such as nonfat milk, cheese, and yogurt. As for eggs, limit yourself to three or four egg yolks a week. Most of the protein in eggs is found in the egg white, anyway.

Nutritional Danger Zones for Vegetarian Strength Trainers

Whether to include or exclude meat in your diet is a matter of personal choice. If you decide to go meatless, then plan your diet carefully to avoid certain nutritional danger zones—namely, iron, zinc, and B12 deficiencies. These deficiencies can hurt exercise performance. Here are some tips for avoiding deficiencies if you're a vegetarian strength trainer.

Get Enough Protein in Your Diet

A challenge for vegetarian strength trainers is to obtain the 1.6 grams of protein per kilogram of body weight required daily to support muscle growth. You can do this by including plenty of low-fat dairy products and protein-rich plant sources in your diet. If you are a pure vegan (you eat no animal foods at all), increase your protein intake to 2.0 grams of protein per kilogram of body weight a day.

Include Some Heme Iron Sources in Your Diet

As noted, all types of animal protein contain the more-easily-absorbed form of iron, heme iron. If you're a semi-vegetarian—that is, still eating fish or chicken but no red meat—you're in luck. Chicken and fish contain heme iron.

Watch the MFP Factor

Meat, fish, and poultry (MFP) also contain a special quality called the MFP factor that helps your body absorb more nonheme iron. When meat and vegetables are eaten together at the same meal, more nonheme iron is absorbed from the vegetables than if the vegetables had been eaten alone. If you're a semi-vegetarian, your body will absorb extra iron from vegetables.

Include Vitamin C Sources

Fruits, vegetables, and other foods that contain vitamin C help the body absorb nonheme iron. For example, if you eat citrus fruits with an iron-fortified cereal, your body will absorb more iron from the cereal than if it had been eaten alone.

Guard Against a B12 Deficiency

Vitamin B12 is one of the most significant nutrients typically missing from the diets of vegans. That's because vitamin B12 is available only from animal products. Fortunately, the body needs only very tiny daily amounts of this vitamin (the RDA is 1.0 microgram for adults), which is used in the manufacture of red blood cells and nerves. Even so, a deficiency is serious, potentially causing irreversible nerve damage.

Fermented food, such as the soybean products miso and tempeh, supplies some vitamin B12 from the bacterial culture that causes fermentation, but generally not enough. Vegans should eat B12-fortified foods or take supplements to ensure a healthy diet.

Watch Iron and Zinc Blockers

Some foods contain phytates, oxalates, or other substances that block the absorption of iron and zinc in the intestine. Coffee and tea (regular and decaffeinated), whole grains, bran, legumes, and spinach are a few examples of foods containing blockers. These foods are best eaten with heme iron sources or vitamin C sources to help your body absorb more iron and zinc.

Consider Iron and Zinc Supplements

Our bodies don't absorb the iron that comes from vegetables as easily as the iron that comes from animal foods. Nonmeat eaters, especially active people or menstruating women, must pay attention to their dietary iron needs.

Animal flesh is the major source of zinc in our diets. So all styles of vegetarian eaters may be at greater risk of having marginally low intakes of this mineral.

Although dietary supplements are not good replacements for food, it may be a good idea to supplement if iron and zinc are in short supply in your diet. Daily supplementation of iron and zinc at the level of 100 percent of the RDA is good insurance against harmful deficiencies.

THE BOTTOM LINE ON PROTEIN

Protein is definitely a key to manufacturing muscle, and the latest research shows that strength trainers who are building muscle, are vegetarians, or do cross-training require slightly elevated amounts of protein. You don't have to go overboard, though, because your body will extract exactly what it needs. By following the recommendations here, you'll get the optimal amount of protein to build muscle and maintain strength.

Sport Nutrition Fact vs. Fiction: Supplemental Amino Acids Build Muscle

Several years ago, researchers at the Centers for Disease Control surveyed 12 popular fitness magazines and found that each contained an average of 26 pitches for muscle-enhancing or energy-releasing products. The researchers also counted the number of products (311) advertised in the magazines, noting that 235 unique ingredients were listed under 89 brands. One out of every three products listed amino acids as ingredients.

Amino acids, sold as free-form amino acids or found in other supplements or powders, are a popular bodybuilding supplement. Because amino acids are endowed with a lot of nitrogen, their use is believed to promote nitrogen retention. Nitrogen retention supposedly enhances the synthesis of proteins by cells, thus leading to muscle growth.

Certain amino acids are being sold as natural anabolics, or muscle-building supplements. They claim to help increase strength and build muscle.

But what about them? Are these claims valid? Will amino acid supplements work for you? Let's take a look at the evidence.

Amino acid supplements that are marketed to strength athletes and exercisers can be classified into two groups: those that stimulate growth hormone (GH) release and those that replenish lost protein from muscles, the branched-chain amino acids (BCAAs).

Much of the hoopla over amino acids has to do with growth hormone, which is naturally produced in the body. GH regulates growth (including muscle growth) and helps release fat from storage for fuel, among other functions. Sleep, exercise training, and stress are among the factors that stimulate the release of GH in the body.

Over the years, clinical studies have surfaced reporting that injections of huge amounts of amino acids boost the secretion of growth hormone. Keep in mind, though, that elevated levels of growth hormone in the body don't necessarily lead to increases in muscle mass.

Besides, supplemental amino acids are taken orally, not intravenously, and thus don't have the same effect as injections. In one series of experiments, subjects took arginine and ornithine in oral doses of up to 20 grams a day. Fewer than 10 percent of the subjects experienced any significant effect, and those who were affected had only modest increases in growth hormone, even when supplementation was combined with a strength-training program.

One study did successfully show that an oral dose of 1,200 milligrams of arginine pyroglutamate and 1,200 milligrams of lysine, taken on an empty stomach, did promote GH secretion. However, there was no muscle-building effect.

Another study administered large enough doses of the amino acid ornithine to stimulate GH secretion. But again, there was no muscle-building effect. Plus, all the participants got sick from the huge doses.

If you're spending a lot of money on arginine and lysine supplements in hope of building more muscle, consider this. A mere three-ounce portion of lean red meat has about 1,700 milligrams of arginine and 2,200 milligrams of lysine. To get the same amount from supplements, you'd have to pop nearly 20 capsules!

As I mentioned previously, the BCAAs (leucine in particular) are sometimes burned for energy during aerobic exercise. This would lead you to believe that supplementation with BCAAs is a good idea. Not really. As a strength trainer, your body starts drawing on BCAAs for fuel during exercise only if you are not eating enough or not taking in sufficient carbohydrates (carbohydrates keep the body from burning up too much of its BCAA supply). In other words, you should be able to get all the BCAAs you need from food. That's easy to do. Each of the following foods contains all the BCAAs you need daily to prevent protein breakdown during aerobic exercise:

- Three ounces of water-packed tuna
- Three ounces of chicken
- One cup of nonfat yogurt
- One cup of cooked legumes

The existing scientific research doesn't support the muscle-building claims for supplemental amino acids. Nor are the short- and long-term risks of supplementation known. Taking amino acids could cause physiological imbalances that may interfere with your body's normal functioning. Given the present state of knowledge, I don't support the use of these supplements.

The best protein you can provide your body comes from food. One of the main reasons for this has to do with absorption. All nutrients are absorbed better when they come from real food. There are substances in foods, which scientists have coined food factors, that help the body absorb and use nutrients. We don't even know what many of these food factors are, but we do know that they aren't found in food supplements.

As for protein, particularly animal protein, it is one of the most easily absorbed foods. Scientific research has found that 95 to 99 percent of animal protein is absorbed and used by the body. Even protein from plant sources is well absorbed. More than 90 percent of the protein from plants is taken up and put to use by the body.

If you eat a variety of proteins (see table 2.2), you don't need to take protein or amino acid supplements. Just one ounce of chicken contains 7,000 milligrams of amino acids. To get that much in a supplement, you might pay $20 for an entire bottle of amino acid supplements!

TABLE 2.2 Good Sources of Protein

Food	Amount	Protein (g)	Calories
Animal foods			
Beef, lean, sirloin, broiled	3 oz.	26	172
Roasted chicken breast (boneless, no skin)	3 oz.	26	140
Sole/flounder, baked or broiled	3 oz.	21	100
Turkey	3 oz.	25	145
Dairy products			
Cheese	1 oz.	8	107
Cottage cheese, 2%	1/2 c	16	101
Egg, boiled	1 lg	6	78
Egg white, cooked	1 lg	4	17
Milk, dried nonfat, instant	1/2 c	12	122
Milk, low-fat, 1%	1 c	8	102
Milk, nonfat	1 c	8	86
Yogurt, low-fat, plain	8 oz.	13	155
Yogurt, low-fat, fruit	8 oz.	11	250

Food	Amount	Protein (g)	Calories
Nuts, seeds, & nut products			
Peanuts, dry roasted	1 oz.	7	166
Peanut butter	2 tbsp	8	190
Pumpkin seeds, dry roasted	1/2 c	6	143
Sunflower seeds, dry roasted, hulled	2 tbsp	3	93
Soy products			
Soybeans, cooked	1/2 c	15	149
Soy milk	1 c	8	79
Tofu	1/2 c	10	94
Vegetables, high-protein			
Beans, black, boiled	1/2 c	8	114
Chickpeas (garbanzos), boiled	1/2 c	7	135
Lentils, boiled	1/2 c	9	115
Beans, pinto	1/2 c	7	117

Chapter 3

CARBOHYDRATE: THE ENERGY SOURCE FOR INTENSE TRAINING

From the oatmeal you eat for breakfast to the baked potato you eat for dinner, carbohydrates are the leading nutrient fuel for your body. During digestion, carbohydrates are broken down into glucose. Glucose circulates in the blood, where it is known as blood sugar, to be used by the brain and nervous system for energy. If your brain cells are deprived of glucose, your mental power will suffer, and because your brain controls your muscles, you might even feel weak and shaky.

Glucose from the breakdown of carbohydrate is converted also to glycogen for storage in either liver or muscle. Two-thirds of your body's glycogen is stored in the muscles, and about one-third is stored in the liver. When muscles use glycogen, they break it back down into glucose through a series of energy-producing steps.

It is no surprise that pasta, cereal, grains, fruit, vegetables, sport drinks, and other carbohydrates are the foods of choice for endurance athletes, who fill up on carbs by carbohydrate loading to improve their performance in competition. But carbohydrate is just as necessary for strength trainers as it is for endurance athletes. The glycogen it provides is the major source of fuel for working muscles. When carbohydrates are in short supply, your muscles get tired and heavy. Carbohydrate is thus a vital nutrient that keeps your mind and muscles powered up for hard training.

THE FORCE BEHIND MUSCLE BUILDING AND FAT BURNING

Among the nutrients, carbohydrates are the most powerful in affecting your energy levels. But they also affect your muscle-building and fat-burning power. It takes about 2,500 calories to build just one pound of muscle. That's a lot of energy! The best source of that energy is carbohydrate. It provides the cleanest, most immediate source of energy for body cells. In fact, your body prefers to burn carbohydrate over fat or protein. As your body's favored fuel source, carbohydrate spares protein from being used as energy. Protein is thus free to do its main job—build and repair body tissue, including muscle.

Carbohydrate is a must for efficient fat-burning, too. Your body burns fat for energy in a series of complex chemical reactions that take place inside cells. Think of fat as a log on a hearth waiting to be

Carbohydrates affect your muscle-building power.

ignited. Carbohydrate is the match that ignites fat at the cellular level. Unless enough carbohydrate is available in key stages of the energy-producing process, fat will just smolder—in other words, not burn as well.

A HIGH-CARB DIET FOR STRENGTH TRAINING

You can create a high-carbohydrate diet by using the Food Guide Pyramid, a practical tool for meal planning developed by the United States Department of Agriculture. There are six categories of foods in the pyramid: the bread, cereal, rice, and pasta group; the vegetable group; the fruit group; the meat, poultry, fish, dry beans, eggs, and nuts group; the milk, yogurt, and cheese group; and the fats, oils, and sweets group. The pyramid illustrates the relative importance of various types of foods.

Every group in the pyramid contains carbohydrate foods. However, because the bread, fruit, and vegetable groups are the richest sources of carbohydrates, those foods are emphasized. Your daily carbohydrate selection should include a variety of carbs from these groups. These foods are loaded with fiber, vitamins, minerals, phytochemicals, and other health-giving nutrients. Here's a closer look.

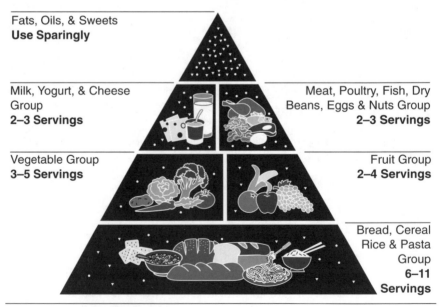

Fats, Oils, & Sweets
Use Sparingly

Milk, Yogurt, & Cheese Group
2–3 Servings

Meat, Poultry, Fish, Dry Beans, Eggs & Nuts Group
2–3 Servings

Vegetable Group
3–5 Servings

Fruit Group
2–4 Servings

Bread, Cereal Rice & Pasta Group
6–11 Servings

USDA Food Guide Pyramid.

Bread, Cereal, Rice, and Pasta

The base of the Food Guide Pyramid is the bread, cereal, rice, and pasta group—all foods from grains. These are the foods that you need each day to maintain health and prevent disease. But according to most surveys, Americans eat very little of these precious foods (21 percent of total calories), compared to the rest of the world. A healthy diet includes at least 6 to 11 servings of grain-type foods every day. One serving of a grain product is equal to one slice of bread, one ounce of ready-to-eat cereal, or one-half cup of a cooked cereal, rice, or pasta.

Along with many fruits and vegetables, the grain group of foods contains complex carbohydrates, which you know best as starches. Starch is to the plant what glycogen is to your body, a storage form of glucose that supplies energy to help the plant grow. At the molecular level, starch is actually a chain of dozens of glucose units. The links holding the starch chain together are broken apart by enzymes during digestion into single glucose units that are circulated to the body's cells.

Friendly Fibers

Also found in the whole grains of complex carbohydrate foods is cellulose. Like starch, cellulose is a branching chain of glucose units. But unlike starch, these chains can't be broken apart by human digestive enzymes. Cellulose is thus an indigestible remnant of food. It passes through the digestive system largely unchanged.

This characteristic gives cellulose an important place in human nutrition. It is a type of fiber that provides dietary roughage to stimulate the action of the digestive tract muscles. Ample fiber in the diet improves elimination.

Whole grain foods contain other fibers besides cellulose such as lignins and hemicelluloses, which can be classified by their solubility in water. Cellulose, lignins, and some hemicelluloses are water insoluble. These fibers do not dissolve in water and are bulk formers. They increase stool volume and weight, and shorten the transit time of food passage through the intestines. Exposure to cancer-causing agents, in food or the by-products of digestion, is thus reduced greatly. Water-insoluble fiber helps improve intestinal regularity and may be an important safeguard against colon cancer. Good grain sources of water-insoluble fiber include whole grains such as wheat, barley, rice, corn, and oats.

Other fiber is water-soluble, including gums, pectins, mucilages, and some hemicelluloses. These fibers can lower cholesterol levels and improve glucose tolerance (the rise and fall of blood sugar). This is also the fiber type that is used in the fiber supplements advertised as diet aids and laxatives. Good sources of water-soluble fibers include oat bran and barley.

Fiber and Fat Loss

The rich fiber content of the whole grain complex carbohydrate foods is a factor in weight control, too, for three reasons. First, high-fiber foods take longer to eat, creating a full, satisfied feeling. Second, they lower levels of insulin, a hormone that stimulates appetite. And third, more energy (calories) is used up during the digestion and absorption of high-fiber foods. There are clearly some real benefits to a high-fiber diet if you are trying to control body fat and stay lean.

Refined vs. Whole Grains

Although primitive humans probably gnawed on whole kernels, today we grind or mill grains to ease their preparation and improve their palatability—thus the term refined grains. Milling subdivides the grain into smaller particles. For example, the whole wheat kernel can be milled to form cracked wheat, fine granular wheat, or even finer whole wheat flour. Refining processes also remove the germ or seed, as well as the bran, a covering that protects the germ and other inner parts of the grain.

When the endosperm, a starch layer that protects the germ, is separated from a corn kernel, you have such products as grits or cornmeal. Another processing technique is known as abrasion, in which the bran of rice or barley is removed and the remaining portion is polished. The result is white rice or pearled barley.

As parts of the kernel such as the germ or bran are removed, so are the nutrients they contain—fiber, unsaturated fat, protein, iron, and several B-complex vitamins. Fortunately, protein, iron, and B vitamins are replaced in cereal products in a process known as enrichment. Enriched cereals are nearly as nutritious as the original grains, so you should not be afraid to include them in your diet. But they do lack the fiber found in whole grains.

As a strength trainer, you're probably used to eating a lot of oatmeal, rice, and other common grains. For variety, you might experiment with some of the more exotic grains now in supermarkets. For instance, tabbouleh, a Middle Eastern dish, is a delicious cold salad made from bulgur wheat. The Russians traditionally use kasha, roasted buckwheat groats, to make both warm and cold dishes and stuffings. Barley makes a hearty soup, and pearled semolina is the traditional variety for making couscous, a Moroccan dish.

Fruits and Vegetables

You've heard it since grade school: Eat your fruits and vegetables, and you'll be healthy. Somewhere between then and now, you may have become skeptical of that advice. It seemed too simplistic. After all, human health and nutrition science must be more complicated than that! But science has put grade school advice to the test and turned up some provocative findings. In a nutshell, the advice you heard as a kid is not only sound, it may be truly life saving.

Thanks to continuing research, there are now more reasons than ever to eat lots of fruits and veggies. In addition to their high vitamin, mineral, and fiber content, fruits and vegetables are chock-full of other nutritional treasures like the following:

- Antioxidants: vitamins and minerals such as vitamin A, beta carotene, vitamins C and E, and selenium that fight disease-causing substances in the body known as free radicals. Antioxidants have some real benefits for strength trainers; see chapter 6 for more details.
- Phytochemicals: plant chemicals that protect against cancer, heart disease, and other illnesses.
- Phytoestrogens: special phytochemicals in tofu and other soy foods that may protect against some cancers, lower dangerous levels of cholesterol, and promote bone building.

The number of servings of fruits and vegetables in your daily diet makes a difference in your well-being. Researchers tracked 832 men, ages 45 to 65, as part of the famous Framingham heart study, which has followed the health of residents of a Boston suburb since 1948. For every increase of three servings of fruits and vegetables that the men ate per day, their risk of stroke decreased by approximately 20 percent. A similar finding was reported previously for women. Those women who ate lots of spinach, carrots, and other vegetables and fruits rich in antioxidant nutrients had a 54 percent lower risk of stroke than other women.

Vegetables are linked to lower risks of other diseases, too. In a study of 120,852 men and women, ages 55 to 69 years, researchers found that those who ate at least a half an onion a day cut in half the risk of developing stomach cancer compared to those who did not regularly eat onions.

Tomatoes and products containing them may protect against prostate cancer. In a diet study sponsored by the National Cancer Institute, researchers identified the carotenoid lycopene as the only one associated with a lower risk of prostate cancer. Tomato sauce, tomatoes, tomato juice, and pizza are primary sources of lycopene, and those individuals who consumed more than 10 servings of these combined foods per week had a significantly decreased risk of developing prostate cancer when compared to those who ate fewer than 1.5 servings per week.

Can you get the same protection from popping supplements? Not exactly. New scientific research has discovered that food factors like antioxidants and phytochemicals work best to fight disease when you get them from food, not when they are isolated as supplements. In other words, a vitamin-mineral supplement, or any other kind of nutritional supplement, can't match the power of eating food.

To get the disease-fighting benefits of fruits and vegetables, you should eat three to five servings of vegetables and two to four servings of fruit every day. One serving of a vegetable is equal to one-half cup cooked or chopped raw vegetables; one cup raw, leafy vegetables; one-half cup cooked legumes; or three-fourths cup vegetable juice. One serving of a fruit is equal to one medium piece of raw fruit, one-half grapefruit, one melon wedge, one-half cup berries, one-fourth cup dried fruit, or three-fourths cup of fruit juice.

Table 3.1 includes a list of carbohydrates that are important in a strength-training diet. Now, let's look at how you can plan your meals to include enough carbohydrates to train at peak levels.

CARBS: HOW MUCH, HOW OFTEN?

Clearly, there are plenty of reasons to fill up on carbohydrates, particularly the complex kind. To support the demands of strength training, I strongly recommend that strength trainers eat a diet in which 70 percent of their total daily calories come from carbohydrates. On a diet of 2,000 calories, at least 1,400 of the calories (70 percent) should come from carbohydrate. There is lots of scientific research to back up my recommendation, including the following study.

TABLE 3.1 Good Food Sources of Carbohydrates for Strength Trainers

Food	Amount	Carbohydrates (g)	Calories
Fruits			
Apple	1 medium	21	81
Orange	1 medium	15	62
Banana	1 medium	28	109
Raisins	1/4 c	29	109
Apricots, dried	1/4 c	25	107
Vegetables			
Corn, canned	1/2 c	15	66
Winter squash	1/2 c	10	47
Peas	1/2 c	13	67
Carrot	1 medium	7	31
Breads			
Whole wheat	2 slices	26	138
Bagel, plain	1 whole (3.5" dia.)	38	195
English muffin	1 whole	26	134
Pita pocket, whole wheat	1 whole (6.5")	35	170
Bran muffin, homemade	1 small	24	164
Matzo	1 sheet	24	112
Granola bar, hard	1 bar	16	115
Granola bar, soft	1 bar	19	126
Low-fat granola bar, Kelloggs	1 bar	29	144
Grains and cereals			
Grape-Nuts	1/4 c	22	97
Raisin Bran	1/2 c	21	86
Granola, low-fat	1/4 c	19	91
Oatmeal, plain, instant	1 packet	18	104
Oatmeal, cinnamon spice, instant	1 packet	35	177
Cream of Wheat, cooked	1 c	27	129

(continued)

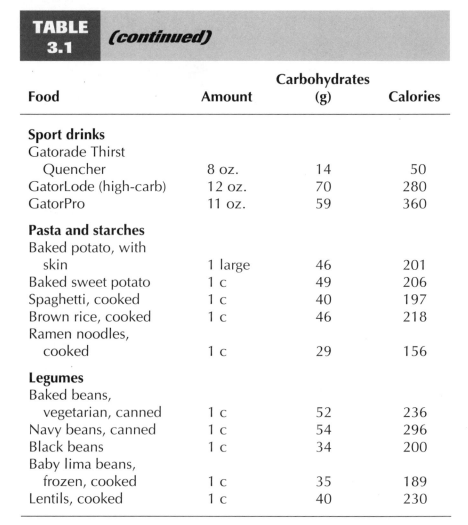

TABLE 3.1 *(continued)*			
Food	**Amount**	**Carbohydrates (g)**	**Calories**
Sport drinks			
Gatorade Thirst Quencher	8 oz.	14	50
GatorLode (high-carb)	12 oz.	70	280
GatorPro	11 oz.	59	360
Pasta and starches			
Baked potato, with skin	1 large	46	201
Baked sweet potato	1 c	49	206
Spaghetti, cooked	1 c	40	197
Brown rice, cooked	1 c	46	218
Ramen noodles, cooked	1 c	29	156
Legumes			
Baked beans, vegetarian, canned	1 c	52	236
Navy beans, canned	1 c	54	296
Black beans	1 c	34	200
Baby lima beans, frozen, cooked	1 c	35	189
Lentils, cooked	1 c	40	230

One group of bodybuilders ate a moderate-protein/high-carbohydrate diet in which 70 percent of the calories were from carbs. A second group followed a high-protein/low-carbohydrate diet in which 50 percent of the calories came from carbs. Before and after each diet, the researchers checked the subjects' muscular endurance (the ability to perform repeated contractions without fatiguing) in their leg muscles. After the diet, the high-carbohydrate group kept going, while the low-carb subjects fizzled out early. The message here: A 70 percent high-carb diet gives you the energy to work out hard, with greater intensity. The harder you work out, the more muscle and power you can build.

Often though, percentages of nutrients don't tell the whole story. Sometimes you have to look at grams of carbohydrate eaten each day. In one study, swimmers were divided into two groups. One group ate a moderate-carbohydrate diet (43 percent of calories from carbs); the other group ate a high-carbohydrate diet (80 percent of calories from carbs). There were no differences in swimming performance between the two groups.

But why not? One explanation may be that all the swimmers were eating high-calorie diets, averaging between 4,000 and 6,075 calories a day. They were all taking in roughly 500 grams of carbohydrate a day. Not only is this ample fuel for strong performance, it's also about as much carbohydrate as muscles will hold. At between 500 to 600 grams of carbohydrate a day, glycogen storage areas in the muscles fill up and won't accept any extra. In other words, there is a ceiling on how much muscle glycogen your body will stock. Think of a gas tank; there are only so many gallons it will hold. Try to fill it with more, and it will only overflow. In fact, once your glycogen stores fill up, the liver turns the overflow into fat, which is stored under the skin and in other areas of the body.

The amount of muscle glycogen you can store depends on your degree of muscle mass. Just as some gas tanks are larger, so are some people's muscles. The more muscular you are, the more glycogen you can potentially store.

To make sure you get the right amount of carbs daily and not too much, determine the number of grams of carbohydrate you need each day. There are two ways to do this. First, if you are on a moderate-calorie diet, your carbohydrate intake should be 70 percent of your total daily calories. Divide the number of carbohydrate calories by 4, since each gram of carbohydrate contributes 4 calories. In a 3,000 calorie diet, 2,100 calories should come from carbs. At least 525 grams of carbohydrate (2,100/4) should be eaten every day. Use a good carbohydrate counter guide to keep track of your carbohydrate intake. Second, if you are on a higher calorie diet, figure your carb intake as follows: consume eight grams of carbohydrate per kilogram of body weight.

Once you up your carbs to the right levels, you should start making additional strength gains. Ample carbs will give you the energy and stamina to push harder and longer for better results in your workout.

CARBOHYDRATES BEFORE AND DURING YOUR WORKOUT

Pre-workout carbs—are they a good idea? It depends. If you're in a mass-building phase and want to push to the max, fuel yourself with carbohydrate before and during your workout. The best timing recommendation for eating before exercise is to eat a low-fat, high-carb meal two to three hours prior to working out. And, of course, you should make sure you are always well hydrated and drink four to eight ounces of fluid immediately before exercise. Following this pattern will ensure that you gain the greatest energy advantage from your pre-exercise meal without feeling full while you exercise.

If you want a little extra boost, try drinking a liquid carbohydrate beverage just before your workout. In a study of strength trainers, one group consumed a carbohydrate drink just before training and between exercise sets. Another group was given a placebo. For exercise, both groups did leg extensions at about 80 percent of their strength capacity, performing repeated sets of 10 repetitions with rest between sets. The researchers found that the carbohydrate-fed group outlasted the placebo group, performing many more sets and repetitions.

Another study turned up a similar finding. Exercisers drank either a placebo or a 10 percent carbohydrate beverage immediately prior to and between the 5th, 10th, and 15th sets of a strength-training workout. They performed repeated sets of 10 repetitions, with three minutes of rest between each set. When fueled by the carb drink (one gram per kilogram of body weight), they could do more total repetitions (149 versus 129) and more total sets (17.1 versus 14.4) than when they drank the placebo. Which all goes to show: Carbs clearly give you an energy edge when consumed before and during a workout. The harder you can work out, the more you can stimulate your muscles to grow.

If you sip a carb drink over the course of a long workout, you can take in too many calories. When counseling clients, I recommend that they alternate between drinking a carb beverage and drinking water during training, especially if their workouts last more than an hour. That way, they don't consume too many calories from the carb drink.

If you're trying to lose body fat, you may want to forgo the pre-workout carb drink. Here's why. Although pre-workout carbs boost

POWER PROFILES

Suppose you want to splurge on treats every so often. Can you do it and not jeopardize your physique goals? Absolutely. A good example is a 38-year-old modern dancer and dance instructor who, like many competitive bodybuilders, needed to stay in reasonably good shape all year round. She indulged herself in occasional splurges such as pizza and desserts, which is perfectly all right, as long as you adjust for your splurge calories. She did this by eating a lower fat, high-carbohydrate lunch whenever she planned to eat a high-fat dinner. That way, the entire day wouldn't be lopsided in favor of fat.

She also liked desserts, so she planned her diet accordingly. Most days during the week, she would eat fruit for dessert. While fulfilling her desire for something sweet after dinner, this plan solved a couple of other nutritional problems. First, it boosted her fiber intake. At the time we met, She was eating a mere 4.5 grams of fiber a day (25 to 35 grams are recommended). Plus, it upped her carb intake, which had been too low (52 percent of total calories) for her activity level and occupation.

your power and stamina, they may keep your body from dipping into its fat reserves for energy. Your entire workout, including aerobics, may run solely on carb fuel and never significantly tap into fat stores for fuel. By working out in a moderately low-carb state (no pre-workout carbs), you can theoretically force your body to start using more fat for fuel.

But there's a tradeoff. You could run low on energy. Although you might choose not to consume any pre-workout carbohydrates, make sure your overall daily diet still contains 65 to 70 percent of its total calories from carbs. Research with strength trainers and other power athletes has consistently shown that performance and energy levels suffer when carb intake dips to around 50 percent of total calories. For more information on how to regulate carbohydrates when you're preparing for competition, see chapter 9.

Consider your goals—mass-building or fat-burning—and listen to your body for signs of fatigue. Adjust your carb intake accordingly, depending on your goals and energy level.

CARB DEPLETION DURING TRAINING

During strength training, glycogen is pulled from storage to replace ATP, the energy compound inside cells that powers muscular contractions. The ATP is broken down in the cells through a series of chemical reactions. The energy released from this breakdown enables the muscle cells to do their work. As you train, the glycogen in your muscles progressively decreases. In fact, you can deplete as much as 26 percent of your muscle glycogen during high-intensity strength training.

Some people might argue that a 26 percent decrease isn't enough to affect strength-training performance. After all, endurance athletes lose as much as 40 percent or more of their glycogen stores during a competitive event. What's the big deal? Well, research has shown that glycogen depletion is localized to the muscles you work. Let's say you train your legs today. What happens is this. During your workout, glycogen depletion occurs mostly in your leg muscles, but not much in your arms, chest, or elsewhere on your body. If scientists measured your glycogen levels after exercise, they might find a 26 percent depletion overall. But your leg muscles could be totally emptied. Hard, intense training depletes glycogen from the individual muscles worked.

REFUELING YOUR MUSCLES AFTER A WORKOUT

After working out, you want your muscles to recover. Recovery is essentially the process of replenishing muscle glycogen. The better your recovery, the harder you'll be able to train during your next workout. There are three critical periods in which to "feed" your muscles with carbs. These three periods are explained in the following discussion.

1. Immediately Following Your Workout

Your muscles are most receptive to producing new glycogen within the first few hours following your workout. That's when blood flow to muscles is much greater, a condition that makes muscle cells practically sop up glucose like a sponge. Muscle cells are also more sensitive to the effects of insulin during this time, and insulin promotes glycogen synthesis. You should therefore take in some carbs immediately after you work out. The question is: What's the best type of carb for refueling?

Answer: carbs with a high glycemic index. The glycemic index is a scale describing how fast a food is converted to glucose in the blood. Foods on the index are rated numerically, with glucose at 100. The higher the number assigned to a food, the faster it converts to glucose. Table 3.2 ranks foods according to their glycemic effect, or rate of conversion. Using this table as a guide, you can see that carbs such as sport drinks, raisins, bananas, or potatoes would be good "refueling" foods.

The rate of conversion is unique for each person and depends on how quickly foods are digested. Digestion speed is affected by the makeup of a particular food. For instance, a greater amount of fiber, protein, and fat content in various foods tends to slow digestion. A good example is ice cream. At a low glycemic index rating of 36, it is broken down very slowly because it contains protein and fat, along with the high glycemic sucrose (sugar).

Because high glycemic index foods replenish glycogen best, you should consume at least 50 grams of these carbohydrates as soon as possible after exercise.

If you're not hungry for food at this time (most of us aren't), polishing off a sport drink is a convenient alternative. It's a great way to refuel with carb calories, as well as rehydrate your body.

A sport drink containing glucose, sucrose, or a glucose polymer (all high on the glycemic index) is a rapid and efficient restorer of glycogen. Some of these drinks may also contain fructose, which isn't as fast at replenishing muscle glycogen as either glucose or sucrose. That being so, try to avoid fructose, including fruit, as the sole source of carbohydrate in the period immediately following your workout. Stick to high glycemic index choices containing glucose and sucrose.

Consuming carbs with protein following a workout has some additional benefits. Be sure to read chapter 7 for more details.

2. Every Two Hours Following Your Workout

Continue to take in high-glycemic carbs every two hours following your workout until you have consumed at least 100 grams within

TABLE 3.2 Glycemic Index of Carbohydrate Foods (Glucose = 100)*

High glycemic	Moderate glycemic	Low glycemic

Beverages
Gatorade–91
Carbonated soft
  drink–68
	Bread and grain products
	Pasta–41
	Rice, white–56
	Rice, brown–55
	Pumpernickel
	  bread–41
	Bran muffin–60
	Popcorn–55
		Fruits
		Apple–36
		Apricots, dried–31
		Bananas, underripe–30
		Grapefruit–25
		Pear–36
		Fructose–23**

Bread and grain products
Bagel–72
Bread, white–70
Bread, whole
  wheat–69
Corn flakes–84
Oatmeal–61
Graham crackers–74
Grape Nuts–67
	Fruits
	Orange juice–57
	Bananas, overripe–52
	Orange–43
	Apple juice,
	  unsweetened–41
		Legumes
		Lima beans–32
		Chickpeas–33
		Green beans–30
		Kidney beans–27
		Lentils–29
		Split peas,
		  yellow–32

Fruits Watermelon–72 Raisins–64 Honey–73**	**Vegetables** Corn–55 Peas–48 Sweet potato–54	**Dairy products** Chocolate milk–34 Skim milk–32 Whole milk–27 Yogurt, low-fat, fruit–33
Vegetables Potato, baked–85 Potato, microwaved–82	**Legumes** Baked beans–48 Lentil soup–44	**Bread and grain products** Barley–25 Power bar–30-35 PR bar–33

*Index based on 50 grams of carbohydrate per serving.

** Not nutritionally the equivalent of fruit.

four hours after exercise and a total of 600 grams within 24 hours after your workout. That equates to roughly 40 to 60 grams of carbohydrate an hour during the 24-hour recovery period.

A word of caution: There is a drawback to high glycemic index foods. They may produce a fast, undesirable surge of blood sugar. When this happens, the pancreas responds by oversecreting insulin to remove sugar from the blood. Blood sugar then drops to a too-low level, and you can feel weak or dizzy.

Low glycemic index foods, on the other hand, provide a more constant release of energy and are unlikely to lead to these reactions. By mixing and matching low and high glycemic foods in your diet, you can keep your blood-sugar levels stable from meal to meal. The watchword here is moderation. Don't overdose on high glycemic index foods or beverages.

3. Throughout the Week

To keep carbohydrate replenishment on track, stay on a high-carbohydrate diet from week to week. An excellent study of hockey players, whose sport requires both muscular strength and aerobic endurance, found that during a three-day period between games, a high-carb diet caused a 45 percent higher glycogen refill than a diet lower in carbs. By consistently fueling yourself with carbs, you can keep your muscles well stocked with glycogen.

You can also supercharge your energy levels. In another study, athletes filled up on carbs for three straight days. They then pedaled at a super-high level of intensity—104 percent of their VO_2max, which describes the ability of the body to take in, transport, and use oxygen. The athletes were able to perform this ride for 6.6 minutes straight, compared to only 3.3 minutes after eating a very low-carbohydrate diet (2.6 percent carbs). So you see, carbs are pure gas for high-intensity exercise.

BODYBUILDING AND CARBOHYDRATE LOADING

Endurance athletes practice a type of nutritional jump start known as carbohydrate loading. Basically, it involves increasing the amount of glycogen stored in the muscle just prior to an endurance competition. With more glycogen available, the athlete can run, cycle, or swim longer before fatigue sets in and thus gain a competitive edge. When done properly, carbohydrate loading works wonders for endurance athletes.

Among strength athletes, bodybuilders have experimented the most with carbohydrate loading. Their goal is not endurance, but bigger muscles. This is generally how they do it. About seven days before the contest, the bodybuilder cuts back on carbs, the depletion stage. Then, a few days before the contest, the bodybuilder starts increasing carb intake, the loading stage. The depletion stage theoretically prepares the muscles to hold more glycogen once more carbs are eaten just prior to competition. With more glycogen, the muscles supposedly look fuller.

But does this actually happen? Not really, says one study. Researchers put nine men, all bodybuilders, on a carbohydrate-loading diet. The diet involved three days of heavy weight training (designed to deplete muscle glycogen) and a low-carb diet (10 percent of the calories were from carbs, 57 percent from fat, and 33 percent from protein). This was followed by three days of lighter weight training (to minimize glycogen loss) and a diet of 80 percent carbohydrate, 5 percent fat, and 15 percent protein. A control group followed the same strength-training program but ate a standard diet. At the end of the study, the researchers measured the muscle girth of all the participants. The results? Carbohydrate loading did not increase muscle girth in any of the bodybuilders.

Of course, this is just one study. Its results should be interpreted cautiously. More information needs to be uncovered about what role, if any, carbohydrate loading plays in preparing for bodybuilding contests. If you're a competitive bodybuilder, you have to be careful with carbohydrate loading, since an excess of carbs in the pre-competition diet can cause water retention.

Your diet should be high in carbohydrate on a daily basis, but this is not carbohydrate loading. Keep in mind, too, that carbohydrate depletion can actually result in the loss of hard-earned muscle.

MENTAL MUSCLE

The amount of carbohydrate in your diet can affect your mental performance. Not only are carbs fuel for muscles, they're also fuel for your brain. On a very low-carb diet, you can feel quite out of sorts—anxious, easily upset, irritable, or depressed. These are all signs of hypoglycemia, too little glucose in the blood.

At Auburn University, researchers put seven female cyclists on three different diets: a low-carb diet (13 percent of calories from carbohydrates); a moderate-carb diet (54 percent of calories from carbohydrates); and a high-carb diet (72 percent of calories from carbohydrates). The cyclists followed each of the three diets for one week at a time. While on the low-carb diet, the cyclists felt tired, tense, depressed, and more likely to get angry.

Mounds of research have shown that carbs do have a positive effect on state of mind. So in a very real sense, sufficient carbs are a natural mood elevator.

GO FOR THE CARBS

The most important dietary factor that will influence your strength-training performance is the amount of carbohydrate in your daily diet. Giving careful thought to what you eat—and making sure you get plenty of carbohydrates—will provide a solid foundation for optimizing both your performance and your health.

Sport Nutrition Fact vs. Fiction: Do Carbs Make You Fat?

In the '90s, several books hit the bookstores claiming that high-carbohydrate diets make you fat and are therefore bad. The authors based this theory on the fact that some people (only about 10 to 25 percent of the population) are insulin-resistant, a condition in which the pancreas oversecretes insulin to maintain normal blood levels of glucose following a high-carbohydrate meal. This oversecretion theoretically causes the carbs to be converted to stored body fat.

There is just no proof that high-insulin levels in the blood will make you fat. As someone who is active, you are already keeping your insulin levels in line. Though the exact mechanism isn't clear, exercise makes muscle cells more sensitive to insulin. For glucose to enter muscle cells, it has to have help from insulin. When insulin gets to the outer surface of a cell, it acts like a key and unlocks tiny receptors surrounding the cell. The receptors open up and let glucose into the cell for use as fuel.

Maintaining muscle tissue through strength training helps normalize the flow of glucose from the blood into muscle cells where it can be properly used for energy.

Should you be worried about eating pasta and bread? No! Insulin resistance affects only a very small percentage of people. Very overweight people, who tend to have blood sugar problems anyway, are most susceptible. If you suspect a blood sugar problem, consult your physician, who should be able to diagnose it and prescribe the proper treatment.

You should be eating a variety of complex carbs like beans and whole grains, in addition to breads and pasta. Even in the unlikely event you are insulin resistant, such a variety minimizes the effects of the condition. Also, staying active helps control body weight and builds muscle tissue, which helps regulate the body's use of glucose.

Insulin and carbohydrates are not the bad guys when it comes to fat—calories are. You gain body fat when you eat more calories than you burn. It's just that simple.

FAT: FINDING THE RIGHT BALANCE

After about an hour of hard, intense exercise, your glycogen supply can dwindle down to nothing. But not so with your fat stores—another energy source for muscles. In contrast to your limited, but ready-to-use glycogen stores, fat stores are practically unlimited. In fact, it's been estimated that the average adult man carries enough fat (about a gallon) to ride a bike from Chicago to Los Angeles, a distance of roughly 2,000 miles.

So if fat stores are nearly inexhaustible, why worry about carb intake and glycogen replenishment? And why not supplement with fat as an extra source of energy?

True, there is certainly a large enough tank of fat on your body to fuel plenty of exercise, and for a long time. (That's one reason why there's no need to supplement with extra fat.) But the problem is that fat can be broken down only as long as oxygen is available. Oxygen must be present for your body to burn fat for energy, but not to burn glycogen. In the initial stages of exercise, oxygen is not yet available. It can take from 20 to 40 minutes of exercise before fat is maximally available to the muscles as fuel. The glucose in your blood and glycogen in your muscles are pressed into service first.

That's not to say fat is hard to burn. It isn't. But how efficiently your body burns fat depends on your level of conditioning. One of the advantages of strength training and aerobic exercise is that your body becomes better accustomed to burn fat as fuel in two major ways.

First, exercise (particularly aerobic exercise) enhances the development of capillaries to the muscles, thus improving blood flow where it's needed. In addition, exercise increases the amount of myoglobin, a protein found in muscles that transports oxygen from the blood into the cells. With better blood flow and greater oxygen to the muscles, your body becomes more efficient at burning fat, which is why you should not neglect the aerobic portion of your training.

Second, exercise stimulates the activity of an enzyme known as hormone sensitive lipase, which promotes the breakdown of fat for energy. The more fat you can break down and burn, the more defined you will look.

Fat is most definitely an exercise fuel, but a second-string source of energy nonetheless. During strength training, your body still prefers to burn carbohydrate for energy, from glucose in the blood or glycogen in the muscles. In fact, one of the main reasons our bodies store fat is not to supply energy for exercise, but rather to help us survive in the event of a long famine or debilitating illness.

Fat is certainly one of the more controversial issues in nutrition. There is so much confusing information in the media about different kinds of fat, and their pros and cons. Let us try to clear up the confusion, once and for all.

A FAT FIGHTER'S PRIMER

There are three major types of fatty material in the body: triglycerides, cholesterol, and phospholipids. Triglycerides, true fats, are the form stored in fat tissue and in muscle. A small percentage of fatty material is found in the blood, circulating as free fatty acids, which have been chemically released from the triglycerides. Of the three types of fatty material, triglycerides are the most involved in energy production. In fact, research with bodybuilders has found that triglycerides do serve as a significant energy source during intense strength training. So not only will strength training help you build muscle, it will help you burn body fat, too.

Cholesterol is a waxy, light-colored solid that comes in two distinctly different forms. You might call the first kind "the cholesterol in the blood," and the second, "the cholesterol in food." Required for good health, blood cholesterol is a constituent of cell membranes and is involved in the formation of hormones, vitamin D, and bile, which is a substance necessary for the digestion of fats. Because your body can make cholesterol from either fats, carbohydrates, or proteins, you don't need to supply any cholesterol from food.

When you eat a food that contains cholesterol, that cholesterol is broken into smaller components that are used to make various fats, proteins, and other substances that your body requires. The cholesterol you eat doesn't become the cholesterol in your blood. While it is important to reduce your intake of high-cholesterol foods, it is even more critical to lower your intake of saturated fat (the kind found mostly in animal foods). That's because the liver manufactures blood cholesterol from saturated fat. The more saturated fat you eat, the more cholesterol your liver makes.

If your liver produces large amounts of cholesterol, the excess circulating in the bloodstream can collect on the inner walls of the arteries. This accumulation is called plaque. Trouble starts when plaque builds up in an artery, narrowing the passageway and choking blood flow. A heart attack can occur when blood flow to the heart muscle is cut off for a long period of time, and part of the heart muscle

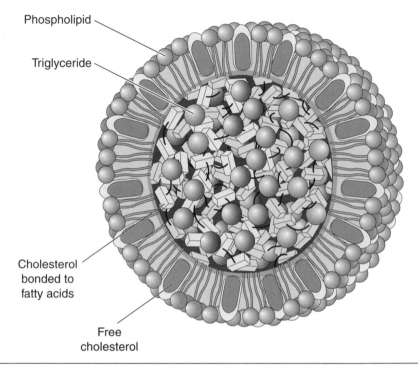

Phospholipid

Triglyceride

Cholesterol
bonded to
fatty acids

Free
cholesterol

A lipoprotein, the transport vehicle for fats and cholesterol in the blood.
Adapted, by permission of The McGraw-Hill Companies, from Gordon M. Wardlaw and Paul M. Insel, 1990, *Perspectives in Nutrition*, 1st ed. (St. Louis: Mosby).

begins to die. High blood cholesterol is therefore a major risk factor for heart disease, but one that can be controlled with exercise and a low-fat diet.

Cholesterol may be present in blood as a constituent of low-density lipoprotein (LDL) or of high-density lipoprotein (HDL). LDL and HDL affect heart disease risk differently. LDL contains the greater amount of cholesterol and may be responsible for depositing cholesterol on the artery walls. LDL is known as bad cholesterol; the lower your blood value, the better.

HDL contains the smaller amount of cholesterol; its job is to remove cholesterol from the cells in the artery wall and transport it back to the liver for reprocessing or excretion from the body as waste. HDL is the good cholesterol; the higher the amount in your blood, the better.

A total cholesterol reading of above 200 may be a danger sign. But what really counts is your ratio of the good HDL cholesterol to the bad LDL cholesterol. Generally, your HDL should be higher than 35, while your LDL should be below 130.

The third type of fatty material, phospholipids, is involved primarily in the regulation of blood clotting. Along with cholesterol, phospholipids form part of the structure of cell membranes.

FOOD FATS

Want to get rid of that extra fat on your body? Then cut down on the fat in your diet. There's no question that the fat you eat turns into body fat more easily than carbohydrates and proteins do. The more fat you eat, the more fat you wear. It's just that easy.

What hasn't been so easy, though, is figuring out how much fat and what kind of fat to eat to stay healthy. Here's a closer look.

Fats from food are chemically classified according to the hydrogen content of the tiny building blocks of fat, their fatty acids, into three groups: saturated, polyunsaturated, and monounsaturated. Saturated fats are usually solid at room temperature and, with the exception of tropical oils, come from animal sources. Beef fat and butter fat are high in saturated fatty acids. Butter fat is found in milk, cheeses, cream, ice cream, and other products made from milk or cream. Low-fat or nonfat milk products are much lower in saturated fat. Tropical oils high in saturated fat include coconut oil, palm kernel oil, and palm oil, and the cocoa fat found in chocolate. They are generally found in commercial baked goods and other processed foods.

Polyunsaturated and monounsaturated fats are usually liquid at room temperature and come from nut, vegetable, or seed sources. Polyunsaturated fats like vegetable shortening and margarine are solid because they have been hydrogenated. Hydrogen has been added to the fatty acids in a process that hardens the fat. The resulting fat is comprised of substances known as trans-fatty acids, which have been linked to unhealthy changes in cardiovascular health. Omega-3 fatty acids are a special kind of polyunsaturated fat found mostly in fish oils from cold-water fish, such as salmon, mackerel, halibut, swordfish, black cod, and rainbow trout, and shellfish. This fat helps prevent abnormal blood clotting which can lead to strokes.

Monounsaturated fatty acids are found in large amounts in olive oil, canola oil, and peanut oil. Monounsaturated fats appear to have a protective effect on blood cholesterol levels. They help lower the bad cholesterol (LDL cholesterol), but maintain the higher levels of good cholesterol (HDL cholesterol).

Essential Fats

Of all dietary fats, only two polyunsaturated fatty acids—linoleic acid and linolenic acid—are considered essential. In other words, your body can't make these fatty acids; you have to get them from food. They are required for normal growth, the maintenance of cell membranes, and healthy arteries and nerves. In addition, essential fats keep your skin smooth and lubricated and protect your joints. They also assist in the breakdown and metabolism of cholesterol. Vegetable fats such as corn, soybean, safflower, and walnut oils are all high in essential fats. So are nuts, seeds, green leafy vegetables like broccoli, and the so-called "fat-fish" from cold waters.

If you slash your fat intake to minuscule levels, or cut it out of your diet altogether, you risk an essential fat deficiency. This is not a widespread problem because Americans get their fill of fat. Even so, I have seen many athletes, bodybuilders in particular, go to extremes in cutting fat. When this happens, the body has trouble absorbing sufficient amounts of the fat-soluble vitamins A, D, E, and K. Furthermore, the health of cell membranes is jeopardized because low-fat diets are low in vitamin E. Vitamin E is an antioxidant that prevents disease-causing free radicals from puncturing cell membranes. Plus, it helps in the muscle repair process that takes place after exercise.

HOW MUCH ESSENTIAL FAT IS ENOUGH?

You can go overboard on fat too. Too much fat in your diet causes weight gain and gradually leads to obesity and related health problems. Excessive saturated fat in the diet can also elevate cholesterol, particularly the dangerous type (LDL cholesterol). On the other hand, polyunsaturated and monounsaturated fats have been shown to cut cholesterol levels. However, polyunsaturates may also lower the protective type of cholesterol known as HDL cholesterol. Very high intakes of polyunsaturated fats have been linked to higher risks of cancer.

So where's the happy medium between too much fat and too little? Exactly how much fat should you eat daily for good health?

According to the American Heart Association, the maximum amount of fat considered healthy in your daily diet is 30 percent or less of the total number of calories you eat. Saturated fat should be 10 percent or less of total daily calories; monounsaturated and polyunsaturated fats should also be at 10 percent or less, preferably with more monounsaturates than polyunsaturates. Dietary cholesterol should be kept to a daily maximum of 300 milligrams or less.

If you're a bodybuilder or strength trainer trying to stay lean, you should lower your total fat intake to 20 percent of total calories each day. Your low-fat diet should contain much more unsaturated than saturated fat: 5 percent saturated, 8 percent monounsaturated, and 7 percent polyunsaturated.

One way to monitor your fat intake is by counting the grams of fat in your diet each day. You can calculate your own suggested daily fat intake by using the following formulas:

Total fat: Total calories × 20% = daily calories from fat/9 calories per g = ___ g total fat
(example: 2,000 calories × .20 = 400/9 = 45 g total fat)

Saturated fatty acids (SFA): Total calories × 5% = daily calories from SFA/9 calories per g = ___ g SFA
(example: 2,000 calories × .05 = 100/9 = 11 g SFA)

Be sure to read food labels for the fat content per serving of the foods you buy in the supermarket. The grams of fat are listed under Nutrition Facts Per Serving on any food package that provides a nutrition label.

Another way to monitor your fat intake is by limiting the majority of foods in your diet to those that have only 20 percent or less of their calories from fat. By using the fat calories per serving information on the nutrition label, you can easily determine if a food meets this criteria. Use the following formula to find percentage of calories from fat:

(Total fat calories per serving divided by total calories per serving) × 100 = % calories from fat

Here's an example of how this formula works:

(54 fat calories divided by 220 calories) × 100 = 24% of calories from fat

If you don't have a head for math and hate counting grams, simply populate your diet with plenty of complex carbs. Fill up on whole grain breads, cereals, pastas, beans, vegetables, and fruits, and eat smaller portions of meats. You'll automatically eat a low-fat diet.

Fat-Fighting Tips

When there is no nutrition information available about a particular food, remember these helpful hints about the sources of fat and cholesterol in foods.

1. The major sources of saturated fats are meats and whole milk dairy products. Choose lean cuts of good or choice grade meat like round, sirloin, and flank, and eat portions that are no larger than the palm of your hand. Chicken, turkey, and fish are always leaner meat choices.

2. When preparing and eating meats, make sure to trim all visible fat and skin, and use cooking racks to bake, broil, grill, steam, or microwave to avoid melting the fat back into the meat.

3. When eating lunch meats, select low-fat or fat-free chicken or turkey breast, rather than high-fat bologna or salami.

4. Dairy foods are very important in your diet. To cut the fats, choose low-fat or nonfat products rather than whole milk, and include them two to three times each day.

5. Cholesterol is found only in animal products, and egg yolks are a concentrated source of cholesterol. Substitute three egg whites and one yolk for two whole eggs, or use egg substitutes. Because meats and dairy products also contain cholesterol, limit egg yolks to three to four a week to maintain a low-cholesterol diet.

6. Processed and prepared foods, especially snack foods, can be very concentrated sources of fat. Hydrogenated vegetable fats may not be any healthier than saturated fats, so pay attention to the total amount of fat in the food. Read labels carefully, even on "lite" products, to determine if they really are lower in fat.

FAT SUBSTITUTES AND FAT REPLACERS

These fake fats are concocted by food technologists who alter the properties of everyday ingredients to make them feel and taste like fat in foods. Fake fats are made from carbohydrates, proteins, and fats.

Carbohydrate-based fats are formulated from starches and fibers. An example is polydextrose, a partially absorbable starch that supplies about one calorie per gram (versus nine calories per gram from fat). Polydextrose is used in frozen desserts, puddings, and cake frostings. A similar product is maltodextrin, a starch made from corn used to replace fat in margarines and salad dressings.

Cellulose and gum are two types of fibers used to manufacture fat replacers. When ground into tiny particles, cellulose has a consistency that feels like fat when eaten. Cellulose replaces some or all of the fat in certain dairy-type products, sauces, frozen desserts, and salad dressings. Gums such as xanthan gum, guar gum, pectin, and carrageenan are used to thicken foods and give them a creamy texture. Added to salad dressings, desserts, and processed meats, gums cut the fat content considerably.

Protein-based fat replacers are formulated from milk or eggs, heated or blended into mist-like particles that feel creamy on the tongue. These fat replacers are found in ice cream, yogurt, sour cream, dips, cheese spreads, salad dressings, mayonnaise, margarine, and butter spreads.

A fat-based fat substitute now on the market is Olestra from Procter & Gamble. Technically, Olestra is a sucrose polyester, meaning a combination of sugar and fatty acids. Your body can't digest Olestra, so it's virtually calorie free. But because of its makeup, some people eating it may get a laxative effect, ranging from mild to severe, depending on how much is consumed. Reports that Olestra may block the absorption of fat-soluble vitamins, beta carotene, and other carotenes forced the FDA to require that all Olestra-containing products be fortified with vitamins A, D, E, and K.

We don't yet know what effect artificial fats have on health. There's a concern among nutritionists and other health advocates that consumers may get so carried away with eating fat-free foods, that they'll eat fewer nutrient-dense food such as fruits, vegetables, and grains.

If you enjoy the new fat-free products, do so in moderation. Current research supports the notion that fat replacers and fat substitutes may help slash total fat in the diet. But the safety of some of the products is still in question—a fact you should consider before using them.

In addition, continue to read nutrition labels and determine the fat content for yourself. Don't rely on the advertising hype on the front of the label. Terms like "lite" or "light" may have nothing to do with the fat content or calorie content of the food. According to the 1993 FDA labeling regulations, the words "light" or "lite" may not be used without qualifying information (such as "lite texture"). "Light" or "lite" may mean that the food is lighter in color, or in flavor, that it is lower in salt, or that it is crispier, but the label must provide this information.

MCT Oil

Processed mainly from coconut oil, medium-chain triglyceride oil (MCT oil) is a special type of dietary fat that was first formulated in the fifties by the pharmaceutical industry for patients who had trouble digesting regular fats. Still used in medical settings, MCT oil is also a popular fitness supplement, marketed as a fat burner, muscle builder, and energy source.

At the molecular level, MCT oil is structured quite differently from conventional fats such as butter, margarine, and vegetable oil. Conventional fats are made up of long carbon chains, with 16 or more carbon atoms strung together, and are thus known as long-chain triglycerides (LCTs). Body fat is also a long-chain triglyceride. MCT oil, on the other hand, has a much shorter carbon chain of only 6 to 12 carbon atoms, which is why it is described as a medium-chain triglyceride.

As a result of this molecular difference, MCTs are digested, transported, and metabolized much more quickly than fatty acids from regular oils or fats, and thus have some interesting properties. To begin with, MCTs are burned in the body like carbohydrates. Unlike conventional fats, MCTs are not stored as body fat but are shuttled directly into the cells to be burned for energy. In fact, MCT oil is burned so quickly that its calories are turned into body heat—a process known as thermogenesis, which boosts the metabolic rate. The higher your metabolism, the more calories your body burns.

Does that mean if you take MCT oil you can rev up your metabolism and therefore burn more fat? Researchers at the University of Rochester looked into this possibility. In an experiment involving seven healthy men at the University of Rochester, they tested whether a single meal of MCTs would increase the metabolic rate more than an LCT meal would. The men ate test meals containing 48 grams of MCT oil or 45 grams of corn oil, given in random order on separate days. In the study, metabolic rate increased 12 percent over six hours after the men ate the MCT meals but increased only 4 percent after LCTs were consumed. What's more, concentrations of triglycerides in plasma (the liquid portion of blood) were elevated 68 percent after the LCT meal, but did not change after the MCT meal. These findings led the researchers to speculate that replacing LCTs with MCTs over a long period of time might be beneficial in weight loss.

Other researchers aren't so sure. In a study at Calgary University in Alberta, Canada, healthy adults were placed on a low-carbohydrate diet supplemented with MCT oil. The researchers found that the diet had no real effect on elevating the metabolism. The calories burned over a 24-hour period were less than 1 percent of total caloric intake. However, there was a decrease in muscle protein burned for energy. While MCT might not be a fat burner per se, it may help preserve lean mass by inhibiting its breakdown.

In most studies on MCT oil and fat burning, volunteers ingest huge amounts of the fat—usually 30 grams or more—to bring on metabolic-boosting results. Such amounts are just not tolerable for most people because too much MCT oil produces intestinal discomfort and diarrhea. In my opinion, taking such huge doses of MCT oil to spur fat burning just isn't practical.

There's another problem with using MCT oil to try to burn fat. The recommended way to take MCT oil is with carbohydrates, a practice that prevents ketosis. In ketosis, by-products of fat metabolism called ketones build up if carbs aren't available to assist in the final stages of fat breakdown. But when MCTs are taken with carbs, there is no effect on fat burning whatsoever. Here's why. Carbs trigger the release of insulin, which inhibits the mobilization of fat for energy. Thus, there's simply no benefit to using MCT oil as a fat-burner. You have to do it the old-fashioned way, by exercising and watching your diet.

Another claim attached to MCT oil is that it helps you put on muscle. But there are no controlled studies to prove this. Using some MCT oil to sneak in extra calories for harder workouts makes some sense, though. Go easy at first by taking one-half a tablespoon to a tablespoon a day. Its fast absorption can cause cramping and diarrhea if you eat too much. Before experimenting with MCT oil, get your doctor's okay.

Sport Nutrition Fact vs. Fiction: The Truth About High-Fat Diets

Many bodybuilders, strength trainers, and exercisers have been experimenting with high-fat diets to lose body fat. Basically, these diets call for a high protein intake (around 25 to 30 percent of total daily calories), low carbs (around 40 percent of total daily calories), and lots of fat (anywhere from 30 to 70 percent of total daily calories). The diets theoretically reduce insulin levels in the body. Insulin is a hormone that, among other functions, promotes fat storage. With low insulin levels, the body supposedly burns more stored fat for energy. As noted in previous chapters, insulin doesn't make you fat. Overeating and underexercising do. Besides, regular exercise and weight control automatically keep insulin levels in line.

High-fat diets are self-defeating for strength trainers. First, they are too low in carbs. When carbs are in short supply in the muscle, the body has no other source of energy it can use to build muscle. Fat cannot be used as fuel for strength-training exercise. Workouts are not as intense, and you can actually lose muscle as a result. Muscle loss compromises your ability to burn fat.

Second, these diets are too high in protein. As noted previously, you don't need an excess of protein to build muscle. And third, high-fat diets tend to be too low in calories. On a diet that supplies an insufficient number of calories, you would lose some fat, but you would also lose hard-earned muscle.

A few more points: You may have heard that a high-fat diet is a good energy booster. This claim is based partly in fact. Research with cyclists has shown that a high-fat diet can extend endurance. But here's the catch. The cyclists didn't have the power to pedal uphill during their daily training rides. So while they had the endurance, they didn't have the oomph. Strength trainers and other athletes need both.

The explanation behind this has to do with muscle fibers. The muscle fibers used in endurance activity are technically known as slow-twitch, or type I. They contract very slowly but can sustain their contractions for long periods without fatiguing. Slow-twitch fibers get most of their energy from burning fat, a process that requires oxygen. The cyclists had good endurance because their slow-twitch muscle fibers had adapted to using fat for fuel.

As for power and strength, that's another story altogether. The muscle fibers used to sprint, lift weights, or power an uphill ride are called fast-twitch, or type II fibers. They contract rapidly but fatigue more easily. Their energy comes from burning glycogen, not fat. They simply can't adapt to using fat for energy. The bottom line: A high-fat diet will sap your strength.

Remember, too, that dietary fat is easily stored as body fat because the fats are chemically similar. Calorie for calorie, fat in the diet turns into fat on the body more easily than carbohydrate. As I've already stated: Eat fat, wear fat.

What's more, following a high-fat diet is playing Russian roulette with your health. Excessive dietary fat is linked to all sorts of life-shortening illnesses, including heart disease and cancer. Steer clear of these fad approaches to dieting and stick to high-carbohydrate fare instead.

Chapter 5

FLUIDS FOR ENERGY AND STAMINA

Quick: What's the most critical nutrient for growth, development, and health? If you guessed "water," congratulations!

The importance of water in the diet is frequently overlooked, and most people don't even consider it an essential nutrient. However, without any water or other fluids, you'll die within a week.

While water does not provide energy in the same way carbs and fat do, it plays an essential role in energy formation. As the most abundant nutrient in your body, it is the medium in which all energy reactions take place. Thus, you need ample fluids for fuel and stamina. You get those fluids from a variety of sources—the foods you eat, the beverages you consume, and the plain, pure water you drink. Here's a closer look at the importance of water and other fluids in the diet.

AN ESSENTIAL NUTRIENT

It is hard to say enough good things about water. It makes up about 60 percent of the body weight in adults. It is involved in all metabolic processes. It carries nutrients throughout the body and transports waste products away. It is a part of the lubricant fluid in your joints to keep them moving. And when your body's temperature begins to rise, water acts like the coolant in your radiator. Enough said! You can see why water is so vital to health.

WATER, WATER EVERYWHERE

Nearly all of the foods you eat contain water, which is absorbed during digestion. Most fruits and vegetables are 75 to 90 percent water. Meats contain roughly 50 to 70 percent water. And beverages such as juice, milk, and sport drinks are more than 85 percent water. On average, you consume about four cups of water daily from food alone.

But that's not enough to keep your body "watered." You need a bare minimum of 8 to 10 cups of pure water daily or about a quart for every 1,000 calories of food you eat—even more to replace the fluid you lose during exercise. Depending on your size and how much you sweat, you lose about a quart (four cups) of water per hour of exercise. If it's hot and humid, you could lose up to two quarts of water in an hour.

THE TEMPERATURE REGULATOR

Your body produces energy for exercise, but only 25 percent of that energy is actually used for mechanical work. The other 75 percent is released as heat. The extra energy produced during exercise causes your body to heat up, raising your core temperature. To get rid of that extra heat, you sweat. As sweat evaporates, your blood and body cool. If you couldn't cool off, you would quickly succumb to the heat stress caused by the increase in your body's core temperature. Thank goodness for water!

WATER AND FAT BURNING

Drinking more water can actually help you stay lean, indirectly. Your kidneys depend on enough water to do their job of filtering waste products from the body. In a water shortage, the kidneys need backup, so they turn to the liver for help. One of the liver's many functions is mobilizing stored fat for energy. By taking on extra assignments from the kidneys, the liver can't do its fat-burning job as well. Fat loss is compromised as a result.

WATER AND EXERCISE PERFORMANCE

Ever wondered why some days you're so pooped you can't pump iron? One reason may be dehydration. To move your muscles, you need water. Of all places in your body, water is found in highest concentration in metabolically active tissues like muscle, and in lowest amounts in relatively inactive tissues such as fat, skin, and some parts of bone. Muscles are controlled by nerves. The electrical stimulation of nerves and contraction of muscles occurs due to the exchange of electrolyte minerals dissolved in water (sodium, potassium, calcium, chloride, and magnesium) across the nerve and muscle cell membranes. If you're low on water or electrolytes, muscle strength and control are weakened. In fact, a water deficit of just 2 to 4 percent of your body weight can cut your strength-training workout by as much as 21 percent if you are dehydrated—and your aerobic power by a whopping 48 percent. Your body's thirst mechanism kicks in when you have lost 2 percent of your body weight in water. But by that time, you are already dehydrated. To prevent dehydration, you must get yourself on a scheduled plan to drink often throughout the day. (See the drinking schedule that follows.)

WATER DEFICIENCY: THE WARNING SIGNS

Most people are walking around in a moderately dehydrated state. Add exercise and a warm climate, and you spell dehydration in a big way. What about you? Are you dehydrated? Table 5.1 lists the early and severe warning signs of dehydration and heat stress.

TABLE 5.1	Symptoms of Dehydration and Heat Stress	
Early signs	**Severe signs**	
Fatigue	Difficulty swallowing	
Loss of appetite	Stumbling	
Flushed skin	Clumsiness	
Heat intolerance	Shriveled skin	
Light-headedness	Sunken eyes and dim vision	
Dark urine with a strong odor	Painful urination	
Dry cough	Numb skin	
	Muscle spasm	
	Delirium	

HOW TO MONITOR

It is easy to monitor yourself for early signs of dehydration.

- Check your urine. It should be light colored with little odor. If it is a golden color or a deep color with a strong odor, you are dehydrated.
- Weigh yourself without clothing before and after exercise. For every pound lost during exercise, you have lost about two cups of fluid. Any weight lost during exercise is fluid loss and should be replaced by fluids as soon after exercise as possible.
- Dehydration is cumulative. Your body can't rehydrate itself. If you fail to rehydrate on consecutive occasions, you will become increasingly dehydrated and begin to suffer from the early symptoms of dehydration.
- Sore throat, dry cough, and a hoarse voice are all additional signs of dehydration.
- A burning sensation in your stomach can signal dehydration.
- Watch for muscle cramps. No one knows for sure what causes muscle cramps, but a shortfall of water may be an important factor. Muscle cramps are more apt to occur if you are doing hard, physical work in the heat and don't drink enough fluids. You can usually alleviate the cramps by moving to a cool place, drinking fluids, and replacing electrolytes with a sport drink.

A DRINKING SCHEDULE FOR STRENGTH TRAINERS

You usually can't rely on thirst to tell you when to drink water. The body's drive to drink is not nearly as powerful as its drive to eat, and the thirst mechanism is even less powerful. By the time your thirst mechanism kicks in during exercise, you've already lost about 1 to 2 percent of your body weight as sweat. You need to drink water at regular intervals, thirsty or not. And you need to do so every day. Remember, if you fail to drink enough water one day, your body can't automatically rehydrate itself the next. You'll be doubly dehydrated and possibly begin to show some signs of dehydration.

For some additional guidelines, read the position stand on exercise and fluid replacement issued by the American College of Sports Medicine. These guidelines appear in the sidebar article.

For workouts, here's a schedule that will keep you well hydrated before, during, and after exercise.

Before Exercise

Drink 8 to 16 ounces (one to two cups) of fluid two hours before exercise. Then, drink four to eight ounces (one-half cup to one cup) of fluid immediately before exercise to make sure the body is well hydrated. In very hot or very cold weather, you need even more water: 12 to 20 ounces (one and one-half to two and one-half cups) of fluid 10 to 20 minutes before exercise. Exercising during cold weather elevates your body temperature, and you still lose water through perspiration and respiration.

During Exercise

Drink four to six ounces every 15 to 20 minutes during exercise; make it eight ounces (one cup) in extreme temperatures. Although this might seem tough at first, once you schedule it into your regular training routine, you will quickly adapt to the feeling of fluid in your stomach. In fact, the fuller your stomach, the faster it will empty. Dehydration slows the rate that your stomach will empty. Make regular water breaks part of your training now.

After Exercise

This is the time to replace any fluid you have lost. Weigh yourself before and after exercise; then drink two cups of fluid for every pound body weight you have lost.

American College of Sports Medicine Position Stand on Exercise and Fluid Replacement

It is the position of the American College of Sports Medicine that adequate fluid replacement helps maintain hydration and, therefore, promotes the health, safety, and optimal physical performance of individuals participating in regular physical activity. This position statement is based on a comprehensive review and interpretation of scientific literature concerning the influence of fluid replacement on exercise performance and the risk of thermal injury associated with dehydration and hypothermia. Based on available evidence, the American College of Sports Medicine makes the following general recommendations on the amount and composition of fluid that should be ingested in preparation for, during, and after exercise or athletic competition:

1. It is recommended that individuals consume a nutritionally balanced diet and drink adequate fluids during the 24-hour period before an event, especially during the period that includes the meal prior to exercise, to promote proper hydration before exercise or competition.

2. It is recommended that individuals drink about 500 milliliters (about 17 ounces) of fluid two hours before exercise to promote adequate hydration and allow time for excretion of excess ingested water.

3. During exercise, athletes should start drinking early and at regular intervals in an attempt to consume fluids at a rate sufficient to replace all the water lost through sweating (i.e., body weight loss), or consume the maximal amount that can be tolerated.

4. It is recommended that ingested fluids be cooler than ambient temperature, between 15° and 22° C, (between 59° and 72° F) and flavored to enhance palatability and promote fluid replacement. Fluids should be readily available and served in

containers that allow adequate volumes to be ingested with ease and minimal interruption of exercise.

5. Addition of proper amounts of carbohydrates and/or electrolytes to a fluid-replacement solution is recommended for exercise events of duration greater than one hour since it does not significantly impair water delivery to the body and may enhance performance. During exercise lasting less than one hour, there is little evidence of physiological or physical performance differences between consuming a carbohydrate-electrolyte drink and plain water.

6. During intense exercise lasting longer than one hour, it is recommended that carbohydrates be ingested at a rate of 30–60 grams per hour to maintain oxidation of carbohydrates and delay fatigue. This rate of carbohydrate intake can be achieved without compromising fluid delivery by drinking 600–1,200 ml per hour of solutions containing 4%-8% carbohydrates (g/100 ml). The carbohydrates can be sugars (glucose or sucrose) or starch (e.g., maltodextrin).

7. Inclusion of sodium (0.5–0.7 g per liter of water) in the rehydration solution ingested during exercise lasting longer than one hour is recommended since it may be advantageous in enhancing palatability, promoting fluid retention, and possibly preventing hyponatremia in certain individuals who drink excessive quantities of fluid. There is little physiological basis for the presence of sodium in an oral rehydration solution for enhancing intestinal water absorption as long as sodium is sufficiently available from the previous meal.

Reprinted, by permission, from Victor A. Convertino, Lawrence E. Armstrong, Edward F. Coyle, Gary W. Mack, Michael N. Sawka, Leo C. Senary, Jr., and W. Michael Sherman, 1996, "American College of Sports Medicine Position Stand: Exercise and Fluid Replacement," *Medicine and Science in Sports and Exercise*, 28(1): i.

BEST SOURCES OF WATER

The easiest way to get water is right from your faucet. But reports of contaminated tap water are of concern to many people—and with good reason. The water supply in many areas contains contaminants such as lead, pesticides, and chlorine by-products that exceed federal limits. A good move is to buy a water purifier, which filters lead and other contaminants from tap water. Some filters attach right to the tap; others can be installed as part of the entire water system. One of the most convenient and economic filtering methods is the filter you can place in a special pitcher and put right in your refrigerator.

Another option is to purchase bottled water, and there are hundreds of brands. The most popular brands contain springwater and mineral water. Springwater is taken from underground freshwater springs that form pools on the surface of the earth. Mineral water comes from reservoirs located under rock formations. It contains a higher concentration of minerals than most other sources.

Another type of bottled water is well water, which is tapped from an aquifer. Well, mineral, and spring waters still may contain some contaminants.

Distilled water is another type of bottled water. It has been purified through vaporization and is then condensed. A drawback of distilled water is that it does not usually contain any minerals. And fluoride, a mineral important for dental health, is missing from many bottled waters.

Some people like seltzer water. This is a sparkling water that is bubbly due to the addition of pressurized carbon dioxide. Many of these products are flavored and contain sucrose or fructose.

Regardless of what type of water you drink, be sure to drink the 8 to 10 cups or more you need daily to stay well hydrated.

IS WATER SUPERIOR TO SPORT DRINKS?

In some cases—yes. For exercise lasting one hour or less, water is still the best sport drink around. The nutrient you most need to replace during and after a workout is water.

Fluid-replacer drinks do have their place, mostly for exercise lasting more than an hour, and especially for use by endurance and ultra-endurance athletes. These products are a mixture of water, carbohydrate, and electrolytes. Electrolytes are dissolved minerals that form a salty soup in and around cells. Electrolytes carry electrical charges that let them react with other minerals to relay nerve impulses, make muscles contract or relax, and regulate the fluid balance inside and

TABLE 5.2	Fluid Replacement Beverage Comparison Chart (per 8 oz. serving)				
Beverage	Carb (%)	Sodium (mg)	Potassium (mg)	Other minerals	Calories
Gatorade	6	110	30	Chloride, phosphorus	50
Exceed	7.2	50	45	Chloride, magnesium, calcium	70
PowerAde	8	55	30	Chloride	70
Allsport	8	55	55	Chloride, phosphorus, calcium	70
10-K	6.3	55	30	Chloride, phosphorus, vitamin C	60
Quickick	7	100	23	Chloride, phosphorus, calcium	67
Endura	6.2	46	80	Chloride, calcium, magnesium, chromium	60
1st Ade	7	55	25	Phosphorus	60
Hydra Fuel	7	25	50	Chloride, phosphorus magnesium, vitamin C, chromium	66
Cytomax	5	53	100	Chloride, magnesium	66

outside cells. In hard workouts or athletic competitions lasting an hour or longer, electrolytes can be lost through sweat. For a comparison of the various ingredients in fluid-replacer products, see table 5.2.

Fluid-replacer drinks do two things: replace water and electrolytes lost through sweat, and supply a small amount of carbohydrate to the working muscles. Most drinks are formulated with about 6 to 8 percent of carbohydrate. The carb is either glucose, a simple sugar; fructose, a fruit sugar; sucrose, ordinary table sugar (a blend of glucose and fructose); maltodextrin, a complex carbohydrate derived from corn; or a combination of these.

Because they contain carbs, these drinks benefit athletes competing in events that last an hour or longer. What happens is this: The carbs in these drinks decrease the use of muscle and liver glycogen stores. During competition, athletes can thus run, bike, or swim longer because the supplemental carbs have spared stored glycogen.

There is no evidence showing that electrolytes improve exercise performance. They are not required in supplemental amounts, unless you have a mineral deficiency identified by your physician or your daily sweat losses total more than 3 percent of your body weight (4.5 pounds in a 150 pound athlete). Ultraendurance athletes are among those who do need to replace electrolytes. But if you are eating a balanced diet rich in fruits and vegetables, you are getting your fill of these minerals.

In addition to their ability to replenish fluids, electrolytes, and carbs, fluid replacers may strengthen your immune system. This amazing news comes from Appalachian State University where researchers put two groups of marathoners on some rather high-intensity treadmill exercise for two and one-half hours. One group drank 25 ounces of a fluid-replacer (Gatorade) 30 minutes before exercise, eight ounces every 15 minutes during exercise, and a final 25 ounces over a six-hour recovery period. The other group replenished fluids on the same schedule but with a noncarbohydrate placebo solution.

The researchers took blood samples from the marathoners and found that the Gatorade drinkers had lower levels of cortisol in their blood than did the other exercisers. Cortisol is a hormone that suppresses immune response. The head of the research team, David Nieman, Ph.D., was quoted in *Runner's World* as saying, "It seems that when blood glucose level stays up, cortisol level stays down, thus immune function remains relatively strong."

Since this is just one study, there are obviously no final and complete answers on the glucose-immunity connection. This research is intriguing, nonetheless.

Fluid replacers are designed primarily for endurance athletes. But for strength trainers who train aerobically—particularly in the heat—they have some value, too. The best time to swill one of these drinks is during an aerobic workout or during any period of exertion, especially if you're exercising or working in hot weather. That's when fluid loss is greater than any other time of the year. You can lose more electrolytes, too, although the concentration of these minerals in sweat gets weaker the more fit you are. You also burn more glycogen working out in the heat—another good reason to quench your body with a fluid replacer.

Where fluid replacers may have an edge over water is in their flavor. A lot of people just don't drink much water because it doesn't taste good. When soldiers participating in a study at the United States Army Research Institute of Environmental Medicine were given the choice of drinking plain chlorinated water, flavored water, or lemon-lime fluid-replacer drinks, most chose the fluid replacers or flavored water over plain water. One way to sneak more water in and still get the flavor is to dilute your fluid replacer if you don't need the carbs.

If you are an avid water drinker and really like water, you will benefit just as much from water as you will from using a sport drink—unless you are exercising more than an hour. But if you don't like water, or tend to avoid it during exercise, try filtered water, which has an improved taste. Or try a sport drink that contains less than 8 percent carbohydrate and some sodium. Another idea is to put some

© Mary Langenfeld

Make regular water breaks a part of your training.

powdered sport drink mix into your water, although the powdered mixes don't taste as good as their premixed counterparts. At the least, if a sport drink encourages you to drink more, it has done its job.

IS JUICE A GOOD SPORTS DRINK?

Juices are a source of fluids. Orange juice, for example, is nearly 90 percent water and full of vitamins and minerals. Although juices count as part of your fluid requirement, you'll feel at your best if you drink your 8 to 10 cups or more of water daily.

There are some cautions to consider regarding juice as a fluid in your training diet. In recent years, there has been a lot of hype surrounding the health benefits of drinking fruit and vegetable juices. The makers of commercial juicing machines claim fresh juices are a panacea for all kinds of ills, from digestive upsets to cancer. But is it better to drink your five servings of fruits and veggies every day than eat them? No way!

In most juices, the pulp has been removed from the fruit or vegetables to make the juice. That means all-important fiber has been subtracted, too, since the pulp is where you find the fiber.

Granted, some juice machines boast that their process keeps the pulp in the juice to retain the important fibers and concentrate the nutrients. But these products usually make a juice so thick that it must be diluted before you drink it, like any concentrated fruit juice. Once you water it down, it is nutritionally the same as the other types of extracted juices, but with a little more fiber.

Freshly squeezed juice is often touted as a better source of nutrients than commercial juices. But commercially prepared juices that are frozen and refrigerated properly are only slightly lower in nutrients than fresh juice. In fact, if you don't buy fresh produce, store it properly at home, and don't drink your freshly squeezed juice immediately, your homemade juice could be lower in nutrients than a well-done commercially frozen or refrigerated brand.

Whether they are cooked, squeezed, dried, or raw, fruits and vegetables need to be a big part of your diet. If using a juice machine as one way of getting in more fruits and vegetables is enjoyable for you, then go for it. But remember the drawbacks, and don't use juice as your only source of fruits and veggies.

If you want to drink juice to rehydrate your body, dilute it with water, by at least twofold. A cup of orange or apple juice plus a cup of water will provide a 6 to 8 percent carb solution, similar to a sport drink formulation. Don't use this combination during exercise, however, because of its fructose content. The body doesn't utilize fructose as well as the combination of sugars in a regular sport drink. Additionally, some people are fructose sensitive and may experience intestinal cramping after drinking juice.

Drink your juice/water drink after exercise instead. The addition of water will speed the emptying of the fluid from your stomach and thus rehydrate your body more rapidly. And the carbohydrate will help replenish glycogen.

ALCOHOL: A DANGER ZONE FOR STRENGTH TRAINERS

It has been a long time since any client has asked me whether drinking beer is a good way to replenish fluids and carbs. But clients frequently ask whether alcohol will hurt their exercise performance. And even more frequently, they want to know whether drinking a little bit of alcohol may actually be heart-healthy. Thanks to an ever-growing body of scientific research and knowledge, here are some answers to those questions, and more.

What's in Alcohol?

Alcohol is a carbohydrate, but it is not first converted to glucose as other carbohydrates are. Instead, it is converted into fatty acids and thus is more likely to be stored as body fat. So if you drink and train, alcohol puts fat metabolism on hold. It is not your friend if you are trying to stay lean.

Pure alcohol supplies seven calories per gram, and nothing else. In practical terms, a shot (1.5 ounces) of 90-proof gin contains 110 calories, and a shot of 100-proof gin contains 124 calories. Beer has a little more to offer, but not much. On average, a 12-ounce can of beer contains 146 calories, 13 grams of carbohydrate, traces of several B-complex vitamins, and depending on the brand, varying amounts of minerals. Light beer and nonalcoholic beer are lower in calories and sometimes carbohydrates. The calorie contents of table wines are all similar. A 3.5-ounce serving of table wine contains about 72 calories, one gram of carbohydrate, and very small amounts of several vitamins and minerals. Sweet or dessert wines are higher in calories, containing 90 calories per two-ounce serving.

What Are Alcohol's Side Effects?

Today, alcohol is the most abused drug in the United States. Ten percent of users are addicted, and 10 to 20 percent are abusers or problem drinkers. Alcohol is a central nervous system depressant. Compared to any other commonly used substance, alcohol has one of the lowest effective dose/lethal dose ratios. In other words, there is a very small difference in the amount of alcohol that will get you drunk and the amount that will kill you. But the reason that more people don't die from alcohol intoxication is that the stomach is very alcohol sensitive and rejects it by vomiting.

Acute alcohol intoxication results in tremor, anxiety and irritability, nausea and vomiting, decreased mental function, vertigo, coma, and death. In large amounts, alcohol causes the loss of many nutrients from the body, including thiamin, vitamin B6, and calcium. Furthermore, chronic alcohol abuse has negative side effects on every organ in the body, particularly the liver, heart, brain, and muscle and can thus lead to cancer and diseases of the liver, pancreas, and nervous system.

Also, don't drink alcohol in any form if you are pregnant. It can cause birth defects.

Drinking alcohol in large amounts can also lead to accidents, as well as social, psychological, and emotional problems.

How Does Alcohol Affect Exercise Performance?

Because alcohol depresses the central nervous system, it impairs balance and coordination and decreases exercise performance. Strength and power, muscle endurance, and aerobic endurance are all zapped with alcohol use. Alcohol also dehydrates the body considerably.

Is Alcohol Really Heart-Healthy?

Research has found that daily consumption of one drink per day can do your heart good by positively affecting the levels of good cholesterol (HDL) in your blood. The higher your HDL levels, the lower your risk of heart disease.

However, excessive alcohol intake increases your chance of developing heart disease. More than two drinks a day can raise your blood pressure and contribute to high triglycerides, a risk factor for heart disease. Drinking large amounts of alcohol on a habitual basis can also cause heart failure and lead to stroke.

Alcohol consumption contributes to obesity, another major risk factor in the development of heart disease. Extra pounds are hard on your heart. The higher your weight climbs, the greater your risk. Being overweight also raises blood pressure and cholesterol levels, which are risk factors themselves.

Is a Drink a Day Good Prevention?

The risks of alcohol outweigh its positives. If you drink alcoholic beverages, do so in moderation, with meals, and when consumption does not put you or others in harm's way. Moderation is defined as no more than one drink per day for women and no more than two drinks per day for men. One drink is 12 ounces of regular beer, five ounces of wine, or one and one-half ounces of 80-proof distilled liquor.

Remember: Exercising, quitting smoking, and lowering your blood cholesterol through a healthy diet are better ways to prevent heart disease, without any added risks.

Sport Nutrition Fact vs. Fiction: Soft Drinks Will Rehydrate the Body

If given the option, many people would choose a soft drink over water to rehydrate themselves following a workout. And who can blame them? Soft drinks taste good, seem to quench thirst, and are generally refreshing.

But they are among the worst choices for rehydration. Soft drinks are laced with huge amounts of sugar—roughly the equivalent of 10 teaspoons per can. Because of their sugar content, soft drinks are absorbed less rapidly than pure water. The sugar in them keeps the fluid in your stomach longer so less water is available to your body. Rather than rehydrating your system, soft drinks can make you feel even thirstier. Also, the sugar can trigger a sharp spike in insulin, followed by a fast drop in blood sugar. This reaction can leave you feeling tired and weak. The sugar in soft drinks is high-fructose corn syrup, which does not replenish glycogen as rapidly as other forms of carbohydrate. Fructose can cause cramps in people who are sensitive to it.

What about no-sugar soft drinks? These beverages contain artificial sweeteners, which remain controversial. All soft drinks are, of course, carbonated, and carbonation produces gas. Who wants a gassy stomach, especially during a workout?

Diluting a soft drink isn't a good option either. Even in a diluted concentration, a soft drink has nothing beneficial to offer. As far as rehydration is concerned, no fluids—including artificially sweetened soft drinks—have yet been proven to do a better job than plain old water.

Chapter 6

STRENGTH-TRAINING SUPPLEMENTS

© Raymond J. Malace

Want to get ripped, shredded, striated, and vascular? Every supplement company says they've got the product for you. You have probably stood in the supplement aisle for hours, reading ingredients and wondering which ones really work. Ads for supplements certainly promise dramatic results.

Scientists have only begun to research the nutritional requirements of muscle building. The research is promising, but the whole story on what works and what doesn't is not in yet.

Among the many pills and potions on store shelves are vitamins and minerals. Quite possibly, you may need extra amounts of both. Research shows that most Americans fall short of the requirements for many key nutrients, including vitamins C, E, B12, folic acid, zinc, and magnesium, which is why a growing number of Americans are turning to supplements. A survey by the Centers for Disease Control and Prevention shows that more than 60 percent of the general population takes supplements daily.

Hard workouts do increase your nutritional needs, as does dieting. That's why you may want to add certain vitamins and minerals to your nutritional arsenal. Keep in mind though, vitamin and mineral supplements should not replace food. Your body can get almost all the nutrients it needs from a balanced diet. What's more, your body absorbs nutrients best from food.

However, if you feel that you would like the insurance, a good move is to take a daily antioxidant multiple containing 100 percent of the daily values for vitamins and minerals. These formulations help you "cover your nutritional bases" and contain nutrients that have special value to strength trainers.

THE ANTIOXIDANTS

There is a lot of excitement in strength sports about antioxidants—beta carotene, vitamin C, vitamin E, and the minerals selenium, copper, zinc, and manganese. Antioxidants help fight free radicals, chemicals produced naturally by the body that cause irreversible damage to cells. Free radical damage can leave your body vulnerable to advanced aging, cancer, cardiovascular disease, and degenerative diseases like arthritis.

Certain environmental factors such as cigarette smoke, exhaust fumes, radiation, excessive sunlight, certain drugs, and stress can increase free radicals. And, ironically, so can the healthy habit of exercise.

No one knows for sure how or why exercise does this, but there are some theories. One has to do with respiration. During respiration, cells pick off electrons from sugars and add them to oxygen to generate energy. As these reactions take place, electrons sometimes get off course and collide with other molecules, creating free radicals. Exercise increases respiration, and this produces more free radicals.

Body temperature, which tends to rise during exercise, may also be a factor in generating free radicals. A third possibility is the increase in catecholamine production during exercise. Catecholamines are hormones released in response to muscular effort. They increase heart rate, let more blood get to muscles, and provide the muscles with fuel, among other functions.

Antioxidants help fight free radicals which may be produced by exercise.

Another source of free radical production is the damage done to the muscle cell membrane after intense exercise, especially "eccentric" exercise, such as putting down a heavy weight or running downhill. This type of training causes muscle injury that results in the production of free radicals which last for several days. The point is, several complex reactions occur with exercise, and each one may accelerate free radical production.

Vitamin E and Exercise

Now here's the exciting news: Antioxidants may reduce exercise-related free radical damage. By far the most promising studies on antioxidants and exercise have centered around vitamin E.

Vitamin E resides in muscle cell membranes. Part of its job is to scavenge the free radicals produced by exercise, saving the tissues from damage. Researchers have put vitamin E's power to the test and discovered that it does work.

In a study conducted by Dr. William Evans of Penn State, subjects age 55 and older were given either a daily 800-milligram vitamin E supplement or a placebo. For exercise, they walked or ran downhill. The clues to whether vitamin E protected their muscles against damage were found in the production of two key substances—neutrophils (a special type of white blood cell) and creatine kinase (an enzyme involved in energizing muscle cells). When production of these substances is down, little muscle repair takes place. Free radicals multiply, inflicting their damage for several days after exercise. Conversely, when production is up, muscles are on the mend, and free radicals are kept in check.

Here's what happened. The vitamin E-supplemented group showed much higher production of neutrophils and creatine kinase than did the placebo group. What this indicates is that vitamin E protected against muscle damage and its aftermath of free radical production.

The study also tested subjects who were 30 years old or younger. These subjects responded similarly, regardless of whether they were given the vitamin E supplement or placebo. Dr. Evans concluded that as people age, their vitamin E levels decrease, but their need for them increases, and that supplements can help. Although the study used 800 milligrams (IU) of vitamin E a day, Dr. Evans believes that 400 IU per day would result in similar benefits.

Other Antioxidants and Exercise

An antioxidant cocktail may help too, especially in preventing oxidative stress, a condition where free radicals outnumber antioxidants, according to a study from the Washington University School of Medicine in St. Louis. For one month, unexercised medical students took high doses of antioxidants daily: 1,000 IU of vitamin E, 1,250 milligrams of vitamin C, and 37.5 milligrams of beta carotene. The doses were divided into five capsules a day. Some of the group took placebos.

Prior to supplementation, the students ran at a moderate pace on a treadmill for about 40 minutes, followed by five minutes of high-intensity running to exhaustion. The same exercise bout was repeated after supplementation.

The researchers discovered that oxidative stress caused by exercise was high prior to supplementation. In other words, there was a lot of tissue damage going on. With antioxidants, there was still some oxidative stress caused by exercise, but it wasn't as great. The researchers concluded that taking antioxidants offered protection against tissue damage.

Most of the research in antioxidant supplementation has been done with endurance athletes. But what about strength trainers? If you work out consistently, you are tearing down a lot of tissue. Not only that, muscles generate free radicals during and after exercise. For these reasons, there may be some benefit for strength trainers to take antioxidant supplements. They can help you protect yourself from the potential onslaught of free radicals.

Most of the people I have worked with eat diets that are deficient in vitamin E and other antioxidants. One of the reasons is that active, health-conscious people typically go on diets that are low in fat, but dietary fat from vegetable oils, nuts, and seeds is one of the best sources of vitamin E. What's more, some active people, particularly strength trainers, are known to limit their intake of fruit. Misinformed, they think the fructose it contains will turn up as body fat on their physiques. But by cutting out fruits, they cut out foods that are loaded with the antioxidants beta carotene and vitamin C.

Antioxidant Supplements and Performance

If you take antioxidants, will you be able to work out longer and harder? Whether antioxidant supplementation really improves performance hasn't been adequately nailed down by research. But if you are undernourished—that is, you have a vitamin deficiency—you will definitely feel better and perform better by correcting that deficiency. But if your diet is already high in antioxidants, supplementing with extra antioxidants may not make much of a difference in your performance.

How Much?

The amounts of vitamin C and beta carotene that seem to be protective are easily obtained from food. To get enough of these two vitamins, follow the U.S. Department of Agriculture's Food Guide Pyramid recommendations. Strive to eat at least three to five servings of vegetables and two to four servings of fruits every day.

As for vitamin E, a supplement of 100 to 400 IUs per day is adequate. To boost your intake of the other antioxidants, be sure your daily vitamin-mineral supplement contains antioxidants.

The functions of the key antioxidants are summarized in table 6.1.

THE B-COMPLEX VITAMINS

In this family of nutrients, there are eight major B-complex vitamins—thiamin, riboflavin, niacin, vitamin B12, pyridoxine, folic acid, pantothenic acid, and biotin—that work in accord to ensure proper digestion, muscle contraction, and energy production. While these nutrients do not enhance performance, training and diet do alter the body's requirement for some of them.

Thiamin

Thiamin helps release energy from carbohydrates. The amount of carbs and calories in your diet determines your dietary requirement for this vitamin. By eating a well-balanced, high-carbohydrate diet, you generally get all the thiamin you need. The best food sources of thiamin are unrefined cereals, brewer's yeast, legumes, seeds, and nuts.

There is one possible exception, however. Are you supplementing with a carbohydrate supplement to increase calories? If so, you may need extra thiamin, particularly if your carb formula contains no thiamin. For every 1,000 calories of carbs you consume from a formula, you need to add 0.5 milligrams of thiamin to your diet.

TABLE 6.1 Key Antioxidants

VITAMINS

Beta carotene

Exercise-related function	May reduce free radical production as a result of exercise and protect against exercise-induced tissue damage; complements the antioxidant function of vitamin E.
Best food sources	Carrots, sweet potatoes, spinach, cantaloupe, broccoli, any dark green leafy vegetable, and orange vegetables and fruits.
Side effects and toxicity	None known because the body carefully controls its conversion to vitamin A. Daily intakes of 20,000 IU from either food or supplements over several months may cause skin yellowing. This disappears when the dosage is reduced.
RDA for adults	No established limits. 2,500 IU daily from supplements is safe. You can get the same amount from a large carrot.

Vitamin C

Exercise-related function	Maintains normal connective tissue; enhances iron absorption; may reduce free radical damage as a result of exercise and protect against exercise-induced tissue damage.
Best food sources	Citrus fruits and juices, green peppers, raw cabbage, kiwi fruit, cantaloupe, and green leafy vegetables.
Side effects and toxicity	The body adapts to high dosages. Dosages higher than 250 mg daily may harm immunity. Dosages between 5,000 mg and 15,000 mg may cause burning urination or diarrhea.
RDA for adults	60 mg a day—the same amount found in 1 medium orange. 100 mg daily for smokers.

Vitamin E

Exercise-related function	Involved in cellular respiration, assists in the formation of red blood cells; scavenges free radicals; protects against exercise-induced tissue damage.

(continued)

TABLE 6.1 *(continued)*

Vitamin E *(continued)*

Best food sources	Nuts, seeds, raw wheat germ, polyunsaturated vegetable oils, and fish liver oils.
Side effects and toxicity	None known.
RDA for adults	10 IU a day for men, 8 IU a day for women—the same amount found in 1 tbsp of safflower oil. Up to 400 IU a day in supplement form is considered safe.

MINERALS

Selenium

Exercise-related function	Interacts with vitamin E in normal growth and metabolism; preserves the elasticity of the skin; produces glutathione peroxidase, an important protective antioxidant enzyme.
Best food sources	Cereal bran, Brazil nuts, whole grain cereals, egg yolk, milk, chicken, seafood, broccoli, garlic, and onions.
Side effects and toxicity	5 mg a day from food has resulted in hair loss and fingernail changes. Higher daily dosages are linked to intestinal problems, fatigue, and irritability.
RDA for adults	70 μg for men; 55 μg for women.

Copper

Exercise-related function	Assists in the formation of hemoglobin and red blood cells by assisting in iron absorption; required for energy metabolism; involved with superoxide dismutase, a key protective antioxidant enzyme.
Best food sources	Whole grains, shellfish, eggs, almonds, green leafy vegetables, and beans.
Side effects and toxicity	Toxicity is rare.
RDA for adults	No more than 3 mg a day.

Zinc	
Exercise-related function	Involved in energy metabolism.
Best food sources	Animal proteins, oysters, mushrooms, whole grains, and brewer's yeast.
Side effects and toxicity	Doses higher than 20 mg a day may interfere with copper absorption, reduce HDL cholesterol, and impair the immune system.
RDA for adults	15 mg for men; 12 mg for women.
Manganese	
Exercise-related function	Involved in metabolism and growth; involved with superoxide dismutase, a key protective antioxidant enzyme.
Best food sources	Whole grains, egg yolks, dried peas and beans, and green leafy vegetables.
Side effects and toxicity	Large dosages can cause vomiting and intestinal problems.
RDA for adults	No more than 5 mg a day.

Dieting and erratic eating patterns can leave some nutritional gaps, too. To be on the safe side, be sure to take a daily multiple that contains 100 percent of the RDA for thiamin or up to two milligrams of the nutrient.

Riboflavin

Riboflavin also helps release energy from foods. Like thiamin, your dietary requirement is linked to your calorie intake. As a strength trainer, you need to consume at least 0.6 milligrams of riboflavin for every 1,000 calories of carbs in your diet.

Some athletes may need even more. Riboflavin is easily lost from the body, particularly in sweat. In a study of older women (ages 50 to 67), researchers at Cornell University discovered that exercise increases the body's requirement for riboflavin. But increasing riboflavin intake did not improve performance. An earlier study at Cornell found that very active women required about 1.2 milligrams of riboflavin a day.

Foods rich in riboflavin include dairy products, poultry, fish, grains, and enriched and fortified cereals. A daily multiple containing 100 percent of the RDA or up to two milligrams of riboflavin will help prevent a shortfall.

Niacin

Like the previously mentioned B-complex vitamins, niacin is involved in releasing energy from foods. The amount you need each day is linked to your calorie intake. For every 1,000 calories you eat daily, you need 6.6 milligrams of niacin, or 13 milligrams for every 2,000 calories. If you are using a carb formula that contains no niacin, make sure you take 6.6 milligrams of niacin for every 1,000 calories that you supplement. The best food sources of niacin are lean meats, poultry, fish, and wheat germ. Taking your multiple every day will help you guard against deficiencies.

Vitamin B12

Vital to healthy blood and a normal nervous system, vitamin B12 is the only vitamin found primarily in animal products. It works in partnership with folic acid to form red blood cells in the bone marrow.

If you are a vegetarian who eats no animal foods, be sure to get enough vitamin B12. Fermented and cultured foods such as tempeh and miso contain some B12, as do vegetarian foods fortified with the nutrient. The safest approach is to supplement with a multiple containing 3 to 10 micrograms of vitamin B12.

Folic Acid

Folic acid is the vitamin that, with B12, helps produce red blood cells in the bone marrow. Found in green leafy vegetables, legumes, and whole grains, it also helps reproducing cells synthesize proteins and nucleic acids.

Folic acid first attracted attention for its role in pregnancy. During pregnancy, folic acid helps create red blood cells for the increased blood volume required by the mother, fetus, and placenta. Because of folic acid's role in the production of genetic material and red blood cells, a deficiency can have far-reaching consequences for fetal development. If the fetus is deprived of folic acid, birth defects can result. So important is folic acid intake to women in their childbearing years that foods are now being fortified with it.

There is renewed excitement over folic acid because of its protective role against heart disease and cancer. The vitamin reduces homocysteine, a protein-like substance, in the tissues and blood. High homocysteine levels have been linked to heart disease. Scientists predict that as many as 50,000 premature deaths a year from heart disease can be prevented if we eat more folic acid.

Recent scientific experiments have revealed that folic acid deficiencies cause DNA damage resembling the DNA damage in cancer cells. This finding has led scientists to suggest that cancer could be initiated by DNA damage caused by a deficiency in this B-complex vitamin. Other studies show that folic acid suppresses cell growth in colorectal cancer. It also prevents the formation of precancerous lesions that could lead to cervical cancer, a discovery that may explain why women who don't eat many vegetables and fruits (good sources of folic acid) have high rates of this form of cancer.

Stress, disease, and alcohol consumption all increase your need for folic acid. You should make sure that you're getting 400 micrograms a day of this vitamin, a level that is found in most multiples.

Pyridoxine

Pyridoxine, also known as vitamin B6, is required for the metabolism of protein. It is also vital in the formation of red blood cells and the healthy functioning of the brain. The best food sources of pyridoxine are protein foods such as chicken, fish, and eggs. Other good sources are brown rice, soybeans, oats, and whole wheat.

The RDA for pyridoxine is 0.016 milligrams per gram of protein. Researchers in Finland found that exercise alters pyridoxine requirements somewhat. They learned this by testing the blood levels of various nutrients in a group of young female university students who followed a 24-week exercise program.

If you're wondering whether your own requirement for pyridoxine falls within safe bounds, rest assured that it probably does. A training diet that contains moderate amounts of protein will give you all the pyridoxine you need. In other words, there is no need to supplement. Besides, large doses (in excess of 50 milligrams a day) can cause nerve damage.

Pantothenic Acid

Pantothenic acid participates in the release of energy from carbohydrates, fats, and protein. Because this vitamin is so widely distributed in foods (particularly meats, whole grains, and legumes), it is rare to find a deficiency without a drop in other B-complex vitamins. They all work as a team.

The safe range of intake for pantothenic acid is four to seven milligrams a day. Exercise does affect pantothenic acid metabolism, but only to a very small degree. By following my strength-training nutrition plan, you'll take in plenty of this vitamin to cover any extra needs you might have from exercise.

Biotin

Biotin is involved in fat and carbohydrate metabolism. Without it, the body can't burn fat. Biotin is also a component of various enzymes that carry out essential biochemical reactions in the body. Some good sources of biotin are egg yolks, soy flour, and cereals. Even if you don't get the 30 to 100 micrograms you need daily from food, your body can synthesize biotin from intestinal bacteria. So there's no reason to supplement with extra biotin.

Together with choline and inositol, two other B-complex vitamins, biotin is often found in lipotropic supplement formulations promoted as fat-burners. But there is no credible evidence that biotin or any other supplemental nutrient burns fat.

Some research shows that biotin levels are low in active people. No one is sure why, but one explanation may have to do with exercise. Exercise causes the waste product lactic acid to build up in working muscles. Biotin is involved in the process that breaks down lactic acid. The more lactic acid that accumulates in muscles, the more biotin that is needed to break it down. But don't rush out to buy a bottle of biotin. There is no need to supplement with this vitamin since your body can make up for any marginal deficiencies on its own.

Some strength trainers are in the habit of concocting raw egg milkshakes. Raw egg white contains the protein avidin. Avidin binds with biotin in the intestine and prevents its absorption. Eating raw eggs on a consistent basis can thus lead to a biotin deficiency. But once eggs are cooked, the avidin is destroyed, and there is no danger of blocking biotin absorption.

OTHER VITAMINS

The fat-soluble vitamins A, D, and K are rarely promoted as exercisers' aids, most likely because they are toxic in large doses. Vitamin A, or retinol, is found primarily in animal sources such as liver, fish liver oils, margarine, milk, butter, and eggs. Vitamin A is involved in the growth and repair of tissues, maintenance of proper vision, and resistance to infection. It also helps maintain the health of the skin and mucous membranes. Massive doses in excess of the RDA can cause nausea, vomiting, diarrhea, skin problems, and bone fragility, among other serious problems. The antioxidant provitamin beta carotene converts to vitamin A in the body on an as-needed basis. Beta carotene is found in dark green leafy vegetables, and yellow and orange fruits and vegetables.

Vitamin D is unique; it is also a hormone your body can manufacture on its own when your skin is exposed to sunlight. Vitamin D promotes strong bones and teeth and is necessary for the absorption of calcium. Milk fortified with vitamin D is one of the best dietary sources of this important nutrient. There is no need to supplement with vitamin D, especially since megadoses can be toxic.

Vitamin K's primary function is to assist in the process of normal blood clotting. It is also required for the formation of other body proteins found in the blood, bone, and kidneys. A vitamin K deficiency is extremely rare, and there is no need for supplementation. The best food sources of vitamin K are dairy products, meats, eggs, cereals, fruits, and vegetables.

The functions of vitamins and their possible roles in exercise performance are summarized in table 6.2.

ELECTROLYTES

The tissues in your body contain fluids both inside cells (intracellular fluid), and in the spaces between cells (extracellular fluid). Dissolved in both fluids are electrolytes, which are electrically charged minerals or ions. The electrolytes work in concert, regulating water balance on either side of the cell membranes. Electrolytes also help make muscles contract by promoting the transmission of messages across nerve cell membranes.

TABLE 6.2 Vitamins

VITAMIN B-COMPLEX	
Thiamin (B$_1$)	
Exercise-related function	Carbohydrate metabolism; maintenance of a healthy nervous sytem; growth and muscle tone.
Best food sources	Brewer's yeast, wheat germ, bran, whole grains, and organ meats.
Side effects and toxicity	None known.
RDA for adults	0.5 mg per 1,000 calories consumed, with a minimum of 1.0 mg daily for a 2,000 calorie diet.
Riboflavin (B$_2$)	
Exercise-related function	Metabolism of carbohydrate, protein, and fat; cellular respiration.
Best food sources	Milk, eggs, lean meats, and broccoli.
Side effects and toxicity	None known.
RDA for adults	0.6 mg per 1,000 calories with a minimum of 1.2 mg daily for a 2,000 calorie diet.
Pyridoxine (B$_6$)	
Exercise-related function	Protein metabolism; formation of oxygen-carrying red blood cells.
Best food sources	Whole grains and meats.
Side effects and toxicity	Liver and nerve damage.
RDA for adults	0.016 mg per gram of protein or 2.0 mg for men and 1.6 mg for women.
B$_{12}$	
Exercise-related function	Metabolism of carbohydrate, protein, and fat; formation of red blood cells.
Best food sources	Meats, dairy products, eggs, liver, and fish.

B_{12} *(continued)*

Side effects and toxicity	Liver damage, allergic reactions.
RDA for adults	2 μg.

Niacin

Exercise-related function	Cellular energy production; metabolism of carbohydrates, protein and fat.
Best food sources	Lean meats, liver, poultry, fish, peanuts, and wheat germ.
Side effects and toxicity	Liver damage, jaundice, skin flushing and itching, nausea.
RDA for adults	19 mg for men; 15 mg for women.

Folic Acid

Exercise-related function	Regulation of growth; breakdown of proteins; formation of red blood cells.
Best food sources	Green leafy vegetables and liver.
Side effects and toxicity	Gastric problems; can mask certain anemias.
RDA for adults	200 μg for men; 180 μg for women and 400 μg during pregnancy.

Biotin

Exercise-related function	Breakdown of fats.
Best food sources	Egg yolks and liver.
Side effects and toxicity	None known.
RDA for adults	30–100 μg.

Pantothenic Acid

Exercise-related function	Cellular energy production; fatty acid oxidation.
Best food sources	Found widely in foods.

(continued)

TABLE 6.2 *(continued)*

Pantothenic Acid *(continued)*

Side effects and toxicity	None known.
RDA for adults	4–7 mg.

OTHER VITAMINS

Vitamin A

Exercise-related function	Growth and repair; building of body structures.
Best food sources	Liver, egg yolks, and whole milk, orange and yellow vegetables.
Side effects and toxicity	Digestive system upset; damage to bones and certain organs.
RDA for adults	1,000 μg for men; 800 μg for women.

Vitamin D

Exercise-related function	Normal bone growth and development.
Best food sources	Sunlight, fortified dairy products, and fish oils.
Side effects and toxicity	Nausea, vomiting, hardening of soft tissues, kidney damage
RDA for adults	5 μg.

Vitamin K

Exercise-related function	Involved in glycogen formation and blood clotting.
Best food sources	Vegetables, milk, and yogurt.
Side effects and toxicity	Allergic reactions, breakdown of red blood cells.
RDA for adults	1 μg per kg of body weight; or 80 μg for men and 65 μg for women.

The two chief electrolytes are sodium and potassium. Sodium regulates fluid balance outside cells, while potassium regulates fluids inside cells.

Sodium in the diet is obtained mostly from salt and processed foods. On average, Americans eat two to three teaspoons of salt every day—far too much for good health. A healthier sodium target is 500 milligrams (the minimum requirement) to 2,400 milligrams per day, or no more than one and one-quarter teaspoons of table salt each day.

Although some sodium can be lost from sweat during exercise, you don't have to worry about replacing it with supplementation. Your usual diet contains enough sodium to replace what was lost. What's more, the body does a good job of conserving sodium on its own.

Severe sodium depletion, however, can occur during ultraendurance events such as triathlons that last more than four hours. Consuming one-half to three-quarters of a cup of a sport drink every 10 to 20 minutes is enough to replenish an endurance athlete's need for sodium. Salt tablets, on the other hand, should never be a consideration. They tend to draw water out of your cells and into your gut, making the situation worse, not better.

Potassium works inside cells to regulate fluid balance. Potassium is also involved in maintaining a regular heartbeat, helping muscles contract, regulating blood pressure, and transferring nutrients to cells.

In contrast to sodium, potassium is not as well conserved by the body. That being the case, be sure to eat plenty of potassium-rich foods, such as bananas, oranges, and potatoes. You need between 1,600 and 2,000 milligrams of potassium a day, which can be easily obtained from a diet plentiful in fruits and vegetables.

To get cut, some competitive bodybuilders use diuretics, drugs that increase the formation and excretion of urine in the body. This is a dangerous practice, since diuretics can flush potassium and other electrolytes from the body. Life-threatening mineral imbalances can occur, and some professional bodybuilders have died during competition as a result of diuretic abuse. I can see no rational reason for taking diuretics for competitive purposes. The potential damage just isn't worth it.

Food First

Always count on food first. Food is your body's best source of nutrients. Take the time to plan a healthy, well-balanced diet full of fruits, vegetables, grains, beans, lean meats, and nonfat dairy foods, and use the diet-planning guidelines in chapter 10. Along with dedicated training, a good diet is your best ticket to building a better body.

OTHER VITAL MINERALS—WHAT THEY MEAN TO STRENGTH TRAINERS

There are several other minerals that could be low in your diet, particularly if you are a competitor. A discussion of these vital minerals follows, and their functions are summarized in table 6.3.

Calcium

Ninety-nine percent of the calcium in your body is stored in your skeleton and teeth. The other 1 percent is found in blood and soft tissues. Calcium is responsible for conducting nerve impulses, helping muscles contract, and moving nutrients into and out of cells. Exercise helps your body better absorb calcium.

The chief sources of calcium in the diet are milk and other dairy products. But almost every strength trainer and bodybuilder I have ever counseled has avoided all dairy products like the plague during pre-competition dieting. These athletes feel that these foods are high in sodium. I say, nonsense. One cup of nonfat milk contains 126 milligrams of sodium and 302 milligrams of calcium. Two egg whites, a popular food in the diet of strength trainers and bodybuilders, contain 212 milligrams of sodium and only 12 milligrams of calcium. Sodium hardly seems to be a problem here, and there is no better low-fat source of calcium than nonfat milk.

So are milk and dairy products really your enemy?

Dedicated training and a good diet are the keys to building a better body.

No. You absolutely need these foods in your diet to maintain good health. With plenty of high-calcium foods, your diet provides the calcium needed to maintain healthy blood calcium levels. If you don't have enough in your diet, your body will draw calcium from bones to maintain blood calcium levels. As more and more calcium is removed from bones, they become brittle and break. The most susceptible areas are the spine, the hip, and the wrist. An exit of calcium from the bones can lead to the bone-weakening disease of osteoporosis.

Female bodybuilders are at particular risk of losing bone calcium. In a study I conducted at the 1990 National Physique Committee (NPC) USA Championships in Raleigh, North Carolina, female bodybuilders recorded their diets, were weighed and fat-measured, and answered questions about their training, nutrition, and health.

TABLE 6.3 Major Minerals and Trace Minerals

MAJOR

Calcium

Exercise-related function	A constituent of body structures; plays a part in muscle growth, muscle contraction, and nerve transmission.
Best food sources	Dairy products and green leafy vegetables.
Side effects and toxicity	Excessive calcification of some tissues; constipation; mineral absorption problems.
RDA for adults	800 mg.

Phosphorus

Exercise-related function	Metabolism of carbohydrate, protein, and fat; growth, repair, and maintenance of cells; energy production; and stimulation of muscular contractions.
Best food sources	Meats, fish, poultry, eggs, whole grains, seeds, and nuts.
Side effects and toxicity	None known.
RDA for adults	800 mg.

Potassium

Exercise-related function	Maintenance of normal fluid balance on either side of cell walls; normal growth; stimulation of nerve impulses for muscular contractions; assists in the conversion of glucose to glycogen; synthesis of muscle protein from amino acids.
Best food sources	Potatoes, bananas, fruits, and vegetables.
Side effects and toxicity	Heart disturbances.
RDA for adults	No RDA; but a minimum requirement of 1,600–2,000 mg and 3,500 for active adults.

Sodium	
Exercise-related function	Maintenance of normal fluid balance on either side of cell walls; muscular contraction and nerve transmission; keeps other blood minerals soluble.
Best food sources	Found in virtually all foods.
Side effects and toxicity	Water retention and high blood pressure.
RDA for adults	No RDA; a recommended safe minimum intake is 2.4 mg daily.

Chloride	
Exercise-related function	Helps regulate the pressure that causes fluids to flow in and out of cell membranes.
Best food sources	Table salt (sodium chloride), kelp, and rye flour.
Side effects and toxicity	None known.
RDA for adults	No RDA; a recommended safe minimum intake is 500 mg daily.

Magnesium	
Exercise-related function	Metabolism of carbohydrates and proteins; assists in neuromuscular contractions.
Best food sources	Green vegetables, legumes, whole grains, and seafood.
Side effects and toxicity	Large amounts are toxic.
RDA for adults	350 mg for men; 280 mg for women.

TRACE	

Iron	
Exercise-related function	Oxygen transport to cells for energy; formation of oxygen-carrying red blood cells.

(continued)

TABLE 6.3 *(continued)*

Iron *(continued)*

Best food sources	Liver, oysters, lean meats, and green leafy vegetables.
Side effects and toxicity	Large amounts are toxic.
RDA for adults	10 mg for men; 15 mg for women.

Iodine

Exercise-related function	Energy production; growth and development; and metabolism.
Best food sources	Iodized salt, seafood, and mushrooms.
Side effects and toxicity	Thyroid enlargement.
RDA for adults	150 μg.

Chromium

Exercise-related function	Normal blood sugar and fat metabolism.
Best food sources	Corn oil, brewer's yeast, whole grains, and meats.
Side effects and toxicity	Liver and kidney damage.
RDA for adults	50-200 μg.

Fluoride

Exercise-related function	None known.
Best food sources	Fluoridated water supplies.
Side effects and toxicity	Large amounts are toxic and can cause mottling of teeth.
RDA for adults	1.5-4.0 mg.

Molybdenum	
Exercise-related function	Involved in the metabolism of fats.
Best food sources	Milk, beans, breads, and cereals.
Side effects and toxicity	Diarrhea, anemia, and depressed growth rate.
RDA for adults	75-250 µg.

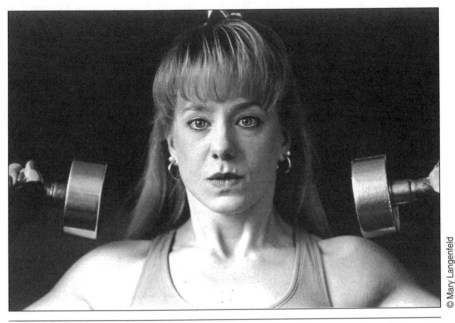

© Mary Langenfeld

Female bodybuilders risk losing bone calcium if they restrict calcium in their diets.

None of the women ate or drank any milk products for at least three months before competition, and most of them never used dairy products at all. Nor did any of these women take calcium supplements.

Eighty-one percent of the women reported that they did not menstruate for at least two months before a contest. The physical stress of training, the psychological stress of competition, the low-calorie diet, and the loss of body fat—these factors can all lead to a decrease in the body's production of estrogen. As in menopause, without enough estrogen, a woman stops menstruating. What's worse, no calcium can be stored in the bone when estrogen levels are low.

Of course, these women were very lean too. On average, they had 9 percent body fat. Extremely low body fat is another risk factor for loss of calcium from bones.

If your dietary practices regarding calcium mirror any of these, you must get calcium back into your diet by eating calcium-rich foods, namely, nonfat milk and dairy products.

If for some reason you cannot or will not drink milk, try nonfat yogurts. They are equally high in calcium, and often do not cause the intestinal problems that some people experience from milk. You can also obtain calcium from alternative sources if you are on a milk-free diet. Table 6.4 lists those sources.

Some people are lactose intolerant, and can't digest milk. They lack sufficient lactase, the enzyme required to digest lactose, a sugar in milk that helps you absorb calcium from the intestine. If you are lactose intolerant, try taking an enzyme product like Lactaid or DairyEase. These products replace the lactase you are missing, and will digest the lactose for you. Another option is Lactaid milk. Available at most supermarkets, Lactaid milk is pretreated with the lactase enzyme.

Calcium supplements may be in order, too. The best supplements are calcium carbonate and calcium citrate malate. Your daily calcium intake should be 1,200 milligrams (women) or 800 milligrams (men) from food and supplements combined. Postmenopausal women need about 1,500 milligrams daily, and women who are pregnant or nursing require between 1,200 and 1,400 milligrams each day. Table 6.5 illustrates how to get a day's worth of calcium from food.

If you have some calcium in your diet, don't take all 1,200 or 800 milligrams of calcium in a supplement. Too much calcium in the diet can cause kidney stones in some people.

A word to women: If you have irregular menstruation, no menstrual cycle, or stop menstruating before a contest, you should see a good sports medicine physician or a gynecologist who is familiar with your sport. Loss of estrogen production at an early age can have a critical impact on your bone health. It is possible to develop osteoporosis at a very early age.

So take care of your inside while you are taking care of your outside. Add some dairy to your diet, and you'll be standing straight and tall for many years to come.

TABLE 6.4	Alternate Sources of Calcium for Milk-Free Diets		

Food	Amount	Calcium (mg)	Calories
Collards, frozen, cooked*	1/2 c	179	31
Soy milk (fortified)	1 c	150	79
Mackerel, canned	2 oz.	137	88
Dandelion greens, raw, cooked*	1/2 c	74	17
Turnip greens, frozen, cooked*	1/2 c	125	25
Mustard greens, frozen, cooked*	1/2 c	76	14
Kale, frozen, cooked*	1/2 c	90	20
Tortillas, corn	2	80	95
Molasses, blackstrap	1 tbsp	176	48
Orange	1 lg	74	87
Sockeye salmon, canned, with bone, drained	2 oz.	136	87
Sardines, canned, with bone, drained	2 med.	92	50
Boston baked beans, vegetarian, canned	1/2 c	64	118
Pickled herring	2 oz.	44	149
Soybeans, cooked	1/2 c	88	149
Broccoli, cooked	1/2 c	36	22
Rutabaga, cooked, mashed	1/2 c	58	47
Artichoke, cooked	1 med.	54	60
White beans, cooked	1/2 c	81	124
Almonds, blanched, whole	1/4 c	94	222
Tofu	2 oz.	60	44

*Frozen, cooked vegetable greens are higher in calcium than fresh cooked greens. If you eat the fresh variety, you have to double your portion to get the same amount of calcium.

Iron

As a strength trainer or bodybuilder, you are constantly tearing down and rebuilding muscle tissue. This process can cause an additional need for iron, a mineral that is enormously essential to

TABLE 6.5 A Healthy Day's Worth of Calcium

Food	Measure	Calcium (mg)	Calories
Orange juice, calcium fortified	1 c	300	112
Nonfat milk	1 c	301	86
Tofu	4 oz.	120	88
Low-fat yogurt, fruit	8 oz.	372	250
Mozzarella cheese, part-skim	1 oz.	229	73
Turnip greens cooked, chopped	1 c	250	50
Total		1,572	659

human health. What's more, there seems to be a common increase in iron losses from aerobic exercises that involve pounding of the feet, like jogging, aerobic dancing, and step aerobics. Also at risk for low iron are women who exercise more than three hours a week, have been pregnant within the past two years, or eat fewer than 2,200 calories a day.

The major role of iron is to combine with protein to make hemoglobin, a special protein that gives red blood cells their color. Hemoglobin carries oxygen in the blood from the lungs to the tissues.

Iron is also necessary for the formation of myoglobin, found only in muscle tissue. Myoglobin transports oxygen to muscle cells to be used in the chemical reaction that makes muscles contract.

When iron is in short supply, your tissues become starved for oxygen. This can make you tire easily and recover more slowly.

The best sources of dietary iron are liver and other organ meats, lean meat, and oysters. Iron is found in green leafy vegetables, too, although iron from plant sources is not as well absorbed as iron in animal protein.

Strength trainers and other active people tend to shy away from iron-rich meats because of their high fat content. But you can beef up the iron in your diet without adding a lot of beef or animal fat. If you don't eat any meat at all, you must pay careful attention to make sure that you get what you need. Here are some suggestions:

1. Eat fruits, vegetables, and grains that are high in iron. You won't get as much iron as from animal foods, but the plant

foods are the lowest in fat. Green leafy vegetables like kale and collards, dried fruits like raisins and apricots, and iron-enriched and fortified breads and cereals, are all good plant sources of iron.

2. Enhance your body's absorption of iron by combining high iron containing foods with a rich source of vitamin C, which improves iron absorption. For example, drink some orange juice with your iron-fortified cereal with raisins for breakfast. Or sprinkle some lemon juice on your kale or collards.

3. Avoid eating very high fiber foods at the same meal with foods high in iron. The fiber inhibits the absorption of iron and many other minerals. Avoid drinking tea and taking antacids with high-iron foods; they also inhibit absorption of iron.

4. Try to keep or add some meat to your diet. Lean red meat, and the dark meat of chicken and turkey are highest in iron. Eating a three- to four-ounce portion of meat three times a week will give your iron levels a real boost. And if you combine your meat with a vegetable source of iron, you will absorb more of the iron from the vegetables.

5. You might need an iron supplement. Fifteen milligrams or 100 percent of the RDA for iron daily may be a big help. Don't pop huge doses of iron, though. The greater the amount of iron taken at one time, the less your body will absorb.

If you think you might be deficient in iron, talk to your physician or a registered dietitian who specializes in sports nutrition. Self-medicating with large doses of iron can cause big trouble and is potentially dangerous.

Zinc

Zinc, one of the antioxidant minerals, is important for hundreds of body processes, including maintaining normal taste and smell, regulating growth, and promoting wound healing.

My research has found that female bodybuilders, in particular, do not get enough zinc in their diets. Zinc is an important mineral for people who work out. As you exercise, zinc is helping to clear lactic acid buildup in the blood. Lactic acid accumulation makes muscles "burn" and eventually brings them to a point of fatigue.

Too much zinc might be a bad thing, however. It has been associated with lower levels of HDL cholesterol (the good kind) in people who exercise.

By eating zinc-rich foods, you can get just the right amount, which is 12 milligrams a day for women and 15 milligrams a day for men. The best sources of zinc are meat, eggs, seafood (especially oysters), and whole grains.

If you restrict your intake of meat, taking a one-a-day multiple will help fill in the nutritional blanks.

Magnesium

Magnesium, a mineral that is in charge of more than 400 metabolic reactions in the body, has been touted as an exercise aid. One study hints at a link between magnesium and muscle strength. A test group of men were given 500 milligrams of magnesium a day, an increase over the RDA of 350 milligrams. A control group took 250 milligrams a day, significantly less than the RDA. After both groups weight trained for eight weeks, their leg strength was measured. The supplemented men got stronger, while the control group stayed the same. But many researchers are not yet convinced that magnesium is a strength builder. They caution that the magnesium status of the subjects prior to the study was unknown. That's an important point, since supplementing with any nutrient in which you are deficient is likely to produce some positive changes in performance and health.

Specifically, magnesium promotes calcium absorption and helps in the function of nerves and muscles, including the regulation of the heartbeat. As I mentioned, the RDA for magnesium for men is 350 milligrams a day. The RDA for women for this important mineral is based upon a value of 4.5 milligrams per kilogram of body weight, with a standard daily recommendation of 280 milligrams for a woman weighing no more than 138 pounds. If you weigh more than 138 pounds, you should figure your magnesium need by using the following formula:

body weight in lbs per 2.2 lbs/kg × 4.5 mg per kg body weight = daily magnesium recommendation (in mg)

The use of laxatives and diuretics can impair magnesium balance. If you use these to make weight, beware that you can compromise your health, and that you risk having nervous system complications from fluid and electrolyte imbalances.

The best dietary sources of magnesium are nuts, legumes, whole grains, dark green vegetables, and seafood. These foods should be plentiful in your diet. You can also supplement these foods with a one-a-day type multiple formulated with 100 percent of the RDA for magnesium.

Quality Control

When you decide which vitamin and mineral supplements you need, stick to brands from well-known manufacturers. Avoid obscure, off brands, or products from unknown international sources. There is so little regulation of the nutritional supplements industry that anything can be, or not be, in the products.

Products from unknown or nonestablished companies may have poor quality control, and may not contain what is stated on the label. Lack of regulatory inspection can also lead to product contamination. These problems are less likely in products manufactured by recognized and well-established food supplement and pharmaceutical companies.

ASPARTATES — A SPECIAL TYPE OF MINERAL SUPPLEMENT

If you perform a lot of aerobic exercise, in addition to strength training, you may be interested in the use of aspartic acid salts for increasing endurance. The potassium and magnesium salts of aspartic acid, an amino acid composed of various substances, are known as aspartates. Aspartate supplements are usually available in health food stores and sport fitness centers.

The feeling of fatigue you get during intense exercise is caused by a combination of factors, and one factor may be the increased rate of ammonia production by the body. Aspartates turn excess ammonia, a by-product of exercise, into urea, which is consequently eliminated from the body.

Studies have shown that potassium and magnesium aspartates increase the endurance of swimming rats. Scientists speculate that the aspartates counteract energy-sapping increases in ammonia concentration.

But what about human exercisers? One study looked into this. Seven healthy men, all competitors in various sports, were tested on a bicycle ergometer. At intervals during a 24-hour period prior to the test, four of the men took a total of five grams of potassium aspartate and five grams of magnesium aspartate. The others took a placebo.

During the test, the men pedaled at a moderately high intensity. The researchers took blood samples prior to, during, and after the test. A week later, the men participated in the same experiment but the conditions were reversed.

In the aspartate-supplemented group, blood ammonia concentrations were significantly lower than in those of the placebo group. Plus, endurance was boosted by about 14 percent in the aspartate group. On average, the aspartate group cycled a total of 88 minutes before reaching exhaustion, whereas the other group cycled about 75 minutes until exhaustion. The researchers noted that "the results of this study would suggest that potassium and magnesium aspartate are useful in increasing endurance performance."

Of course, this is only one study, and aspartates have not been widely researched in exercise science. Supplementing may or may not be useful. If you want to try it, proceed with caution. Excess potassium or magnesium in the system may lead to water retention and mineral imbalances.

Sport Nutrition Fact vs. Fiction: Chromium and Muscle Building

The mineral chromium has been hyped as a safe alternative to anabolic steroids and as a muscle-building agent.

Is there some hard fact behind the hype? Let's take a look.

Chromium is an essential trace mineral that helps the hormone insulin do one of its main jobs—transport glucose into cells. Chromium is also involved in the cellular uptake of amino acids. Its advocates say increased doses of chromium can thus stimulate a higher than normal uptake of amino acids, increasing the synthesis of more muscle mass. But that is quite a leap of faith. The exact way chromium works in the body is not entirely known.

What we do know about chromium is that you can lose it in urine as a result of exercise. In addition, a diet overloaded with simple sugars can force chromium from the body, too. However, the very small quantities of chromium we need for good health can be easily obtained from a good diet. Dietary sources include brewer's yeast, whole grain cereals, meats, raw oysters, mushrooms, apples with skins, wine, and beer.

As for whether chromium supplementation (namely chromium picolinate) builds muscle mass, the evidence is conflicting. Some studies show that it does, others show it does not, and still others show no change. Most of the studies to date have been very poorly designed; they used inaccurate methods of measuring body composition, and they failed to assess chromium status prior to the research.

The best and most well-controlled study to date was conducted several years ago at the University of Massachusetts. Thirty-six football players were given either a placebo or 200 micrograms of chromium picolinate daily for nine weeks during spring training. During that period, they worked out with weights and ran for aerobic conditioning. Before, during, and after supplementation, the researchers assessed the players' diet, urinary chromium losses, girth of various body parts, percentages of body fat and muscle, and strength. Percentages of body fat and muscle were measured by underwater weighing, one of the most precise ways to measure body composition. The results of this study showed that chromium supplementation did not help build muscle, enhance strength, or burn fat.

Some words of warning about supplementation. Chromium picolinate is a mixture of chromium and picolinic acid, a substance that helps the body better use chromium. Picolinic acid, however, has been reported to alter the shape of cells and interfere with their function. What's more, it causes the body to excrete other trace minerals and interferes with the metabolism of iron. Given these drawbacks, and the fact that chromium picolinate doesn't live up to its claims, supplementation is walking a nutritional tightrope at best.

Chapter 7

REPLACING STEROIDS: NATURAL WAYS TO JUICE UP

© Terry Wild Studio

You train hard. You are building body-hard muscle. Still, you want to know: Isn't there something besides intense workouts and healthy food that can help you make gains a little faster, something that will give you a muscle-building edge, with less effort?

Definitely. There are several things you can do to pack on lean muscle. Unfortunately, not all of them are safe—or legal. Anabolic steroids, though approved for medical use and available by prescription only, are among the most abused drugs among athletes. "Anabolic" means "to build," and anabolic steroids tend to make the body grow in certain ways. They do have muscle-building effects, but they are dangerous and life threatening. Once practiced mainly by elite athletes, anabolic steroid abuse has spread to recreational and teen athletes and is now a national health concern. Research shows that among teenagers, 40 percent of kids under age 15 have tried anabolic steroids. Table 7.1 lists some of the dangers associated with these drugs.

In addition to steroids, athletes use other types of drugs including stimulants, pain killers, diuretics, and drugs that mask the presence of certain drugs in the urine. Synthetic growth hormone (GH) is used by athletes as well, because they believe it will increase strength and

TABLE 7.1   Health Dangers of Anabolic Steroids

Liver disease	Masculinization in women
High blood pressure	Muscle spasms
Increased LDL cholesterol	Headache
Decreased HDL cholesterol	Nervous tension
Fluid and water retention	Nausea
Suppressed immunity	Rash
Decreased testosterone	Irritability
Testicular atrophy	Mood swings
Acne	Heightened or suppressed sex drive
Gyncomastia	Aggressiveness
Lowered sperm count	Drug dependence

muscle mass. GH has many horrible side effects, including progressive overgrowth of body tissues, coronary heart disease, diabetes, and arthritis. GH is one of more than 100 drugs that has been banned by the International Olympic Committee. The full list of banned substances appears in table 7.2. Notice that not one of these substances is nutritional; they are drugs and not food substances.

Here's the good news. Forget health-destroying drugs. There are some natural aids you can use to enhance muscle building, give you an extra edge in training, and generally keep your body in healthy balance. Most involve dietary manipulations; some require the use of special supplemental products. Here is a roundup of those aids, from high-calorie supplementation to creatine, that will help you develop your physique and improve your performance in the gym.

HIGH-CALORIE, HIGH-CARBOHYDRATE NUTRITION

The single most important nutritional factor affecting muscle gain is calories, specifically calories from carbohydrates. Building muscle requires an intense, rigorous strength-training program. A tremendous amount of energy is required to fuel this type of exercise—energy that is best supplied by carbs. A high-carbohydrate diet allows for the greatest recovery of muscle glycogen stores on a daily basis. This ongoing replenishment lets your muscles work equally hard on successive days. Studies continue to show that high-calorie, high-carbohydrate diets give strength-trained athletes the edge in their workouts. Here is the bottom line: The harder you train, the more muscle you can build.

To build a pound of muscle, add 2,500 calories a week. This means introducing extra calories into your diet. Ideally, you must increase your calories by 500 to 1,000 a day. But do this gradually, so you don't gain too much fat. What I suggest to strength trainers in a building phase is to start by introducing only 300 to 350 calories a day for a while. Then after a week or two, increase to 500 calories a day. As long as you are not gaining fat, start introducing 1,000 extra calories into your diet daily.

TABLE 7.2 — Drugs Banned by the International Olympic Committee

DRUGS

Stimulants

Amfepramone; Amfetaminil; Amiphenzole; Amphetamine; Benzphetamine; Caffeine; Cathine; Chlorphentermine; Clobenzorex; Clorprenaline; Cocaine; Cropropamine; Crothetamide; Dimetamfetamine; Ephedrine; Etafedrine; Ethamivan; Etilamfetamine; Fencamfamin; Fenetylline; Fenproporex; Furfenorex; Mefenorex; Methamphetamine; Methoxypenamine; Methylephedrine; Methylphenidate; Morazone; Nikethamide; Pemoline; Pentetrazol; Phendimetrazine; Phentermine; Phenylpropanolamine; Pipradol; Prolintane; Propylhexedrine; Pyrovalerone; Strychnine and related compounds

Narcotic analgesics

Alphaprodine; Anileridine; Buprenorphine; Codeine; Dextromoramide; Dextropropoxyphen; Dihydrocodeine; Dipipanone; Ethoheptazine; Ethylmorphine; Heroin; Levorphanol; Methadone; Morphine; Nalbuphine; Pentazocine; Pethidine; Phenazocine; Trimeperidine and related compounds

Anabolic steroids

Bolasterone; Bondenone; Clostebol; Dehydrochlormethyltestosterone; Fluoxymesterone; Mesterolone; Methenolone; Methyltestosterone; Nandrolone; Norethandrolone; Oxandrolone; Oxymesterone; Oxymetholone; Stanozolol; Testosterone and related compounds

b-Blockers

Acebutolol; Alprenolol; Atenolol; Labetalol; Metoprolol; Nadolol; Oxprenolol; Propranolol; Sotalol and related compounds

Diuretics

Acetazolamide; Amiloride; Bendroflumethiazide; Benzthiazide; Bumetanide; Canrenone; Chlomerodin; Chlorthalidone; Diclofenamide; Ethacrynic acid; Furosemide; Hydrochlorothiazide; Mersalyl; Spironolactone; Triamterene and related compounds

Peptide hormones and analogues

Chorionic gonadotrophin; Corticotrophin; Growth hormone; Erythropoietin

A high-calorie, high-carbohydrate diet gives strength trainers an edge.

© Raymond J. Malace

Most of these additional calories should come from carbohydrates in the form of food and liquid carbohydrate supplements. An example of 1,000 calories worth of carbs from food is two cups of pasta, two bagels, and two bananas. It just doesn't take that much additional food to up your carbs.

To be really exact, you can match your carb intake to your weight. As a strength trainer who wants to build muscle, you should take in about nine grams of carbohydrate per kilogram of body weight a day. If you are an athlete who cross trains with strength training and you want to build, figure about 10 grams of carb per kilogram of body weight a day.

Supplementing with liquid carbs is an excellent way to increase those calories. Plus, it appears to support muscle growth. In a landmark experiment, competitive weightlifters took a liquid high-calorie supplement for 15 weeks. The goal of the study was to see how the supplement affected the athletes' weight gain, body composition, and strength. The weightlifters were divided into three groups: those using the supplement and no anabolic steroids, those using the supplement plus anabolic steroids, and a control group taking no supplements or steroids but participating in exercise. The supplement contained 540 calories and 70.5 grams of carbohydrate, plus other nutrients.

All the participants followed their usual diets. The supplement-plus-steroid group and the control group ate most of their calories from fat rather than carbs (45 percent fat, 37 percent carbohydrate). The supplement-only group ate more carbs and less fat (34 percent fat, 47 percent carbs). What's more, the supplement-only group ate about 830 more calories a day than the controls and 1,300 more calories a day than the supplement-plus-steroid group.

Here is what happened. The weight gain in both supplemented groups was significantly greater than in the controls. Those in the supplement-only group gained an average of seven pounds; those in the supplement-plus-steroid group, 10 pounds; those in the control group, three and a half pounds. Lean mass in both of the supplement groups more than doubled, compared to the control group. The supplement-only group lost 0.91 percent body fat, while the supplement-plus-steroid group gained 0.50 percent body fat. Both the supplement-only and supplement-plus-steroid groups gained strength—equally.

These results are amazing, really. They prove that ample calories and carbs are essential for a successful strength-training and muscle-building program. Even more astounding is the fact that you can potentially attain the same results with diet alone as you can with drugs. That is powerful news for drug-free strength trainers everywhere. In chapter 10, you will learn how to plan your own high-calorie, high-carbohydrate diet to support muscle growth.

CARBOHYDRATE/PROTEIN SPORT DRINKS

There is more to the carbohydrate supplementation story. Unimaginable as it may seem, it is within your control to retool your body for more lean muscle and less fat—and do it naturally—all with a simple formulation. Here's how. Immediately following your workout, drink a liquid carb supplement that contains protein, and you will jump-start the muscle-building process, plus boost your energy levels.

This simple formula is 11 ounces of carbohydrates and protein in liquid form taken immediately following your strength-training routine. This is the time your body is best able to use these nutrients for muscle firming and fat burning. The supplement I use with my clients is a Gatorade product, GatorPro. Convenient to take to the gym for a quick refresher after your workout, GatorPro provides 360 calories, 59 grams of carbohydrate, 17 grams of protein, and 7 grams of fat. Be sure to drink it cold. It tastes better that way. You can use any of the meal-replacement drinks on the market.

If you would rather drink your carb-protein supplement at home, try my homemade muscle-building formula. Simply mix a packet of Carnation Instant Breakfast with eight ounces of skim milk, one medium banana, and one tablespoon of peanut butter, and blend until smooth. One serving gives you 414 calories, 17 grams of protein, 70 grams of carbohydrate, and 10 grams of fat.

For a long time now, I have used this formula or GatorPro with many of my bodybuilding clients and soon started observing some major shifts in their body composition, from less fat to more muscle.

How It Works

But why? How does this formula help muscles get stronger and firmer? Exercise, of course, is the initial stimulus. You challenge your muscles by working out, and they respond with growth. But for muscle building to take place, muscles need protein and carbs in combination to create the right hormonal climate for muscle growth.

What happens is this. Protein and carbohydrates trigger the release of the hormones insulin and growth hormone in your body. Insulin is a powerful factor in building muscle, and in many other functions. It helps ferry amino acids into cells, reassembles those amino acids into body tissue, and prevents muscle wasting and tissue loss.

Growth hormone increases the rate of protein production by the body, spurring on muscle-building activity. It also promotes fat burning. Both hormones are directly involved in muscle growth. So you see, your body is primed for growth, thanks to this simple muscle-gain formula.

Scientific Proof

Exploding research into the effect of carb-protein supplements on athletes and exercisers supports what I have observed for years. Some examples follow:

- In one scientific study, 14 normal-weight men and women ate test meals containing various amounts of protein, 0 grams (a protein-free meal), 15.8 grams, 21.5 grams, 33.6 grams, and 49.9 grams, along with 58 grams of carbohydrate. Blood samples were taken at intervals following the meal. The protein-containing meals produced the greatest rise in insulin, compared to the protein-free meal. This study points out that protein clearly has an insulin-boosting effect.

- In another study, nine experienced male strength trainers were given either water (which served as the control), a carbohydrate supplement, a protein supplement, or a carbohydrate/protein supplement. The men took their designated supplement immediately after working out and again two hours later. Right after exercise and throughout the next eight hours, the researchers drew blood samples to determine the levels of various hormones in the blood, including insulin, testosterone (a male hormone also involved in muscle growth), and growth hormone.

The most significant finding was that the carbohydrate/protein supplement triggered the greatest elevations in insulin and growth hormone. Clearly, the protein works hand in hand with postexercise carbs to create a hormonal climate that is highly conducive to muscle growth.

More Energy

If you supplement with a carb/protein beverage after your workout, you will notice something else. That "something else" is higher energy levels. Not only does this nutrient combination stimulate hormone activity, it also starts replenishing muscle glycogen. That means more muscle energy. The harder you can work out, the greater your muscular gains.

When protein is added to the supplement mix, your body's glycogen-making process accelerates faster than if you just consumed carbs by themselves.

Some intriguing research proves this point. In one study, nine men cycled for two full hours during three different sessions to deplete their muscle glycogen stores. Immediately after each exercise bout and again two hours later, the men drank either a straight carb

Research shows protein and carbohydrates help trigger muscle growth.

supplement, a straight protein supplement, or a carbohydrate/protein supplement. By looking at actual biopsies of the muscles, the researchers observed that the rate of muscle glycogen storage was significantly faster when the carb/protein mixture was consumed.

Why such speed? It is well known that eating carbs after prolonged endurance exercise helps restore muscle glycogen. When protein is consumed along with carbs, there is a surge in insulin. Biochemically, insulin is like an acceleration pedal. It races the body's glycogen-making motor in two ways. First, it speeds up the movement of glucose and amino acids into cells, and second, it activates a special enzyme crucial to glycogen synthesis.

CREATINE

Quite probably, creatine is the most important natural performance-enhancing supplement yet to be discovered for strength trainers. Unlike a lot of supplements, creatine has been extensively researched. Exciting experiments show that creatine produces significant improvement in sports that require high levels of strength and power, including strength training, rowing, and cycling sprints. Another big plus for creatine: Several creatine supplementation studies have shown gains in strength and power, and body mass gains averaging two to four pounds or more in one week. Some of this initial weight gain is water that accumulates inside the muscle cells joined with the added creatine. But an increase in cell water is the first step in the anabolic process of muscle building. This, combined with greater strength and power, and higher intensity workouts, leads to more muscle.

Not a Gimmick

Creatine received the following endorsement from a review article in the *International Journal of Sport Nutrition*, a respected publication in sports nutrition. "Creatine should not be viewed as another gimmick supplement; its ingestion is a means of providing immediate, significant performance improvements to athletes involved in explosive sports."

Sound good? You bet. Who wouldn't prefer a bona fide natural supplement like creatine over synthetic, dangerous compounds like steroids? Creatine is the ticket to greater strength and improved muscularity.

How It Works

Creatine is a substance produced in the liver and kidneys—at a rate of about two grams a day—from arginine, glycine, and methionine, three nonessential amino acids. About 95 percent of the body's creatine travels by the blood to be stored in the muscles, heart, and other body cells. Inside muscle cells, creatine is turned into a compound called creatine phosphate (CP). CP serves as a tiny energy supply, enough for several seconds of action. CP thus works best over the short haul, in activities like strength training that require short, fast bursts of activity. CP also replenishes your cellular reserves of ATP, the molecular fuel that provides the power for muscular contractions. With more ATP around, your muscles can do more work.

You load creatine into your muscles, just like endurance athletes do with carbs. Consequently, you can push harder and longer in your workouts because creatine boosts the pace of energy production in your muscle cells. Creatine supplementation does not build muscle directly. But it does have an indirect effect. You can work out more intensely, and this translates into muscle gains.

How Much?

Creatine supplements clearly swell the ranks of creatine in your muscles. This gives a boost to the working muscles' fuel source, glycogen from carbohydrates. The question is, how much creatine do you need? You do get creatine from food—roughly one gram a day. But that is not enough to enhance strength-training performance. You need more.

Creatine usually comes in a powdered form as creatine monohydrate. Scientific research shows that taking 20-25 grams of creatine monohydrate in four or five, five-gram doses (five grams is about a teaspoon) will do the trick. After that, two grams a day—about half a teaspoon—will keep your muscles saturated with enough extra creatine.

The logic that if a small dose is good, a large dose is better, isn't a good idea. The body has a ceiling on the amount of creatine that it will store in the muscles. If you keep taking more, creatine will not continue to load into the muscles. The only known side effect associated with creatine intakes of one to ten grams per day is water weight gain. One report suggests that some people may experience muscle cramping, and possibly muscle tearing when supplementing with creatine. However, these claims are without studies and are unsupportable. While loading with creatine, make sure to **drink extra water**. This may control the cramping. And you're asking for trouble if you belt down daily dosages of 40 grams or more. Such high doses may cause possible liver and kidney damage, according to some reports. Check with your physician before supplementing with creatine.

Supercharge: Creatine with Carbs

Here is an important, newly discovered fact about creatine supplementation. Creatine works best in combination with a liquid carbohydrate supplement. In fact, this combination boosts the amount of creatine accumulated in muscles by as much as 60 percent!

That is the key finding of a recent study. Investigators divided 24 men (average age was 24) into experimental and control groups. The control group took a total of 20 grams of creatine monohydrate a day (five grams of creatine in sugar-free orange juice four times a day) for five days. The experimental group took the same four doses of creatine monohydrate followed 30 minutes later by 17 ounces of a solution containing carbs. Muscle biopsies taken following the five-day test period showed that both groups had elevated creatine levels—but with one dramatic difference. Creatine levels in the experimental group were 60 percent higher than in the control group. The investigators also found higher concentrations of insulin in the muscles of the experimental group.

The implications of this study to strength trainers, athletes, and exercisers are enormous. Just think: By supplementing with creatine and carbs at the same time, you are supercharging your body. With more creatine in your muscles, you have more power to strength train.

The fact that the creatine/carb combo increases insulin is equally important. Insulin increases the uptake of glucose, which is ultimately stored as glycogen in the liver and muscles for fuel. The more glycogen you can stockpile, the more energy you'll have for exercise—including aerobics. The creatine/carb combo is a bona fide energy booster for all types of exercise activity.

WEIGHT-GAIN POWDERS

You've seen them: huge cans brightly labeled with alluring product descriptions like "weight gainer," "solid mass," "lean mass enhancer," or "muscle provider." These products belong to a group of supplements known as weight-gain powders. Most contain various concoctions of carbohydrate, protein, amino acids, vitamins, minerals, and other ingredients thought to enhance performance. The

POWER PROFILES

A 54-year-old strength trainer I know has always described himself as a "hard gainer." Although he has lifted weights for 35 years, it is difficult for him to pack on additional mass. In an effort to jump-start his progress, he decided to try two supplementation techniques—creatine and a carb-protein shake taken immediately following his workouts. Before beginning this program, he took circumference measurements of his arms, legs, and chest.

For two weeks, he took 20 grams of creatine monohydrate divided into four, five-gram doses a day. This dosage has been found to boost creatine content in the muscles by up to 25 percent. Usually, he would mix the creatine in carb shakes, or carb-protein shakes, taken throughout the day. After the two-week loading cycle, he reduced his dosage to 10 grams a day, divided into two five-gram servings taken with a shake. Additionally, he made sure to drink a liquid carb-protein supplement immediately following his workout.

In training, he felt the benefits immediately. His energy levels were higher—and rising with each workout. He had so much stamina that he often felt like working out beyond his normal one-hour training session. Soon he began to break plateaus in his bench press. For the first time ever, he broke the 155-pound barrier and reached 185 pounds on the bench press.

Best of all, he increased his muscular weight (as measured by calipers) from the low 180s to an all-time high of 195. He felt he looked "fuller." His most impressive gains were in his arms, which measured 16 inches (up from 15.24 inches). In 35 years of training, he says he had never made such huge gains until he tried this supplementation program. It truly did give him the jump start he needed.

manufacturers of these products claim that their specific formulations will help you pack on muscle.

But do they? Actually, no one knows for sure. But in 1996, a group of researchers at the University of Memphis put two weight-gain powders to the test. One powder was Gainers Fuel 1000, a high-calorie supplement that adds about 1,400 calories a day to the diet (60 grams of protein, 290 grams of carbohydrate, and 1 gram of fat).

Although the supplement contains many other ingredients, it is formulated with two minerals that have been hyped as muscle builders: chromium picolinate and boron.

Chromium picolinate's link to muscle growth has to do with the fact that it increases the action of insulin, a muscle-building hormone. But that is where the association ends. There is no valid scientific evidence that chromium directly promotes muscle building. (For more on chromium picolinate, see chapter 6.)

Boron has been touted as a supplement that promotes muscle growth, too, by increasing the amount of testosterone circulating in the blood. But experiments have failed to verify this claim. In one recent study, 10 male bodybuilders took two and one-half milligrams of boron daily for seven weeks, while nine male bodybuilders took a placebo. Both groups performed their regular bodybuilding routines for the entire seven weeks. The results were interesting. Lean mass, strength, and testosterone levels increased in all 19 men to the same relative degree. Boron supplementation did not make a bit of difference. It was the training, pure and simple, that did the trick.

Back to the study on weight-gain powders: The second supplement investigated was Phosphagain. It adds about 570 calories a day to the diet (67 grams of protein, 64 grams of carbohydrate, and 5 grams of fat). Like most weight-gain powders, Phos-phagain contains lots of other ingredients that are rumored to build muscle. Among the most notable are creatine (see the previous section), taurine, nucleotides, and L-glutamine. An amino acid found in muscles, taurine has been found in animal studies to enhance the effectiveness of insulin. Nucleotides are the building blocks of RNA and DNA; the nucleotides in Phosphagain are derived from the RNA in yeast. Nucleotides are fundamental to metabolism and integral to the cell division and replication involved in growth and development. As for L-glutamine, an amino acid, it theoretically regulates the water volume in cells and the protein-making process in muscles.

To check the effects of Gainers Fuel 1000 and Phosphagain on muscle growth, the University of Memphis researchers selected 28 strength-trained men, all about the same age (average age was 26). None was currently taking anabolic steroids, nor did any have a history of steroid use. The subjects had been training for an average of six years.

The researchers assigned the men to one of three groups: (1) a third of the men took a maltodextrin supplement three times a day (maltodextrin is a carbohydrate derived from corn); (2) a third took two servings of Gainers Fuel 1000 daily according to the manufacturer's directions; and (3) the remaining third took three servings a day of Phosphagain, according to the manufacturer's directions.

The subjects took their supplements with their morning, midday, and evening meals. None knew which supplement he was taking. They all continued their normal workouts and diets during the course of the study. Additionally, they were told not to take any other supplements for two weeks prior to the study and until the study was over.

Before, during, and after the study, the researchers analyzed the subjects' body composition using some of the most accurate and sophisticated technologies available. This was a very well-designed and well-controlled study.

Here's a summary of what the researchers discovered:

- Both the maltodextrin supplement and the Gainers Fuel 1000 promoted modest gains in muscle mass in combination with a strength-training program.

- In the group that supplemented with Gainers Fuel 1000, fat weight and percent body fat increased significantly.

- Phosphagain supplementation was more effective in promoting muscle gains than either maltodextrin or Gainers Fuel 1000 during strength training. In fact, muscle gains were "significantly greater" with Phosphagain, according to the researchers. The men who supplemented with Phosphagain did not gain any additional fat.

Now before you draw your own conclusions, let me emphasize that it is still up in the air as to exactly which ingredients in Phosphagain were responsible for these results. More tests are needed on weight-gain powders in general, as well as on the individual ingredients they contain to confirm these findings. But, carbs with some protein (weight-gain powders contain both), taken at the proper times, are important supplements to a muscle-building diet. Also, the creatine in Phosphagain could have been a factor in the results.

CARNITINE

Found in red meat and other animal products, carnitine is a protein-like substance once thought to be an important vitamin. Now scientists know carnitine is not an essential nutrient, since the liver and kidneys can synthesize it without any help from food. Most people consume between 50 milligrams and 300 milligrams of this nutrient a day from food. Even if you don't eat that much, your body can produce its own from the amino acids lysine and methionine. About 98 percent of the body's carnitine is stored in the muscles.

Carnitine's main job in the body is to transport fatty acids into cells to be burned as energy. Because of this role, many theories have been floated regarding carnitine's potential benefit to exercisers. One theory is that carnitine boosts exercise performance by making more fat available to working muscles, thus sparing glycogen. Another theory has it that carnitine, because of its role in cellular energy processes, reduces the buildup of waste products like lactic acid in the muscles, thereby extending performance.

Theories aside, what does scientific research show? There have been a lot of studies on carnitine, mostly with conflicting results. In a review article discussing 13 studies on carnitine supplementation, nine studies found that carnitine had no effect on elevating fatty acid levels, increasing aerobic capacity ($\dot{V}O_2max$), or enhancing performance. Only four studies did show effects.

Carnitine is one of those iffy supplements. If carnitine supplementation improves aerobic performance—which some studies say it does—then you could exercise aerobically with greater intensity and thus potentially burn more body fat. That's a big "if," but I see no real danger in trying carnitine—but no real benefits either. According to research, there are no ill effects with doses ranging from 500 milligrams a day to six grams a day for up to a month. However, there is no reason to believe that more than two grams a day makes any difference. Large doses can cause diarrhea.

A word of caution. Some supplement preparations contain a mixture of L-carnitine and D-carnitine. The L-carnitine form appears to be safe. D-carnitine, on the other hand, can cause muscular weakness and excretion of myoglobin, the oxygen-transporting protein in muscle. So if you supplement with carnitine, use products that contain L-carnitine only.

Herbs: Help or Hype?

Herbs are history's most popular self-prescribed medication. They now come in capsules, tablets, liquids, and powders. Americans spend almost $700 million a year on them, and herbs are highly promoted as bodybuilding supplements. Yet there is little evidence that they can help you, and they may even do harm.

An herb is a plant or a part of a plant valued for its medicinal qualities, its aroma, or its taste. Herbs and herbal remedies have been around for centuries. Even Neanderthal man used plants for healing purposes. About 30 percent of all modern drugs are derived from herbs.

Natural, but Not Always Safe

It is a common but dangerous notion to think that because herbs are natural, they are safe. What separates plant-derived drugs from herbal supplements is careful scientific study. Makers of herbal supplements in the United States are not required to submit their products to the Food and Drug Administration (FDA), so there is no regulation of product quality or safety. Without the enforcement of standards, you have a meager chance that the contents and potency described on labels are accurate.

Herbs are classified as food supplements by the FDA. Labeling them as medicines would require stringent testing to prove their safety and effectiveness. This costs millions of dollars per herb, an investment few manufacturers are willing to make.

Fortunately for consumers, supplements can no longer be labeled with unsubstantiated claims. The latest government regulations require that the supplement industry abide by the same labeling laws that govern packaged foods. This means that any supplement bearing a health claim must support the claim with scientific evidence that meets government approval. Any product marketed as a way to cure, modify, treat, or prevent disease is regulated as a drug by the FDA.

It is not uncommon to have an allergic reaction to drugs, even though these medicines have been tested and manufactured with strict safeguards. Therefore, it is even more likely that untested herbs, which are consumed in large amounts, may also produce allergic reactions. These reactions can sometimes be fatal.

Herbs can interact with prescribed medications, too. If you are taking any medications, you should consult your physician, pharmacist, or dietitian before using any herbal supplement.

Pregnant and nursing mothers should avoid all herbal preparations. Ask your physician or dietitian about specific herbal teas, since even these can cause harmful reactions to a developing baby or nursing infant.

Don't give herbal supplements or remedies to children, either. There is virtually no medical information about the safety of herbs for children. Your best intentions could be terribly harmful.

Because there is no quality control regulation of the industry, the danger of chemical contamination of herbal supplements is real. Were the plants sprayed with any chemicals prior to harvesting or processing? Other toxic contaminants may enter the product during processing as well. Products from other countries that are purchased by mail order are even more questionable.

What's on the Market?

The following is a rundown of well-known herbs, either sold alone or found in fitness supplements as part of the formulation. Keep in mind that most of these herbs are medically unproved.

Ephedra (Ma Huang)

Ma Huang, a short-acting stimulant also known as ephedra, is the world's oldest known cultivated plant. Ephedra is found in many herbal remedies marketed for weight loss, making it a popular supplement for bodybuilders, exercisers, and athletes. However, the central nervous system side effects such as nervousness, agitation, and rapid heartbeat make it an ineffective product for many users. When abused, ephedra and its active compound ephedrine can be lethal.

Ginseng

Found in teas and as powders, capsules, extracts, tablets, and ginseng-flavored soft drinks, ginseng has a reputation as an aphrodisiac, an adaptogen (builds resistance to physical stress), a fat burner, an anabolic, and an antioxidant. There is no proof that ginseng enhances sexual performance or potency. There is some evidence that it may positively influence stress. Animal studies show some tissue-building reaction to ginseng taken orally; however, researchers have been unable to replicate those results in humans. There is no compelling research that has yet demonstrated the ability of ginseng to enhance athletic performance.

Guarana

If you see herbal supplements that promise pep and vitality, they probably contain guarana, a dry paste made from crushed plant seeds. Marketed as an energy-giving aid, guarana is a stimulant because it contains high levels of caffeine. A few guarana pills will give you the same kick as a 50-cent cup of coffee.

Mate

Another caffeine-containing herb, mate comes as a tea. It is also advertised as a natural pep producer. But any stimulating effects are only the result of the herb's 2 percent caffeine content.

Precautions

If you are still curious and want to try an herbal supplement, do it with care by following these few precautions. Start with low doses. More is not necessarily better and could be dangerous. Take only one type of supplement at a time. Allow at least 24 hours in between supplements before changing the dosage or starting something new. Keep empty bottles on hand for a while; in case of an adverse reaction, you can provide information about the supplement to your doctor.

CAFFEINE

Caffeine, a drug consumed in coffee, tea, soda, or over-the-counter pharmaceutical preparations, can have a wide range of effects, depending on your sensitivity to it. You might feel alert and wide awake, or get the jitters. Your heart might race, or you might race to the bathroom, since caffeine is a diuretic.

Caffeine lingers in the body, so even small amounts can accumulate over time. It has a half-life of four to six hours—meaning that it takes that long for the body to metabolize half the amount consumed. Because of its half-life, caffeine can become counterproductive. If you drink small amounts during the day, these add up, and you eventually reach a point at which your body has more caffeine than it can handle. As a consequence, by increasing anxiety or restlessness, caffeine reduces the body's ability to function. Other unwanted side effects include stomach upset, irritability, and diarrhea.

Caffeine also inhibits the absorption of thiamin, a vitamin important for carbohydrate metabolism, and several minerals, including calcium and iron. In fact, women who consume caffeine regularly (two or more cups a day) and have a low intake of calcium in their diet (below 600 milligrams a day) may run a greater risk of developing osteoporosis, or brittle bone disease.

In the United States, about 52 percent of all adults drink beverages containing caffeine each day. Many are athletes and exercisers who believe that caffeine can enhance performance. For the most part, studies have shown that caffeine does have some value, although its performance-enhancing effects are as unpredictable as its physical effects.

How It Works

Most of the research with caffeine has focused on endurance sports. The main finding is that for many endurance athletes, caffeine may extend performance.

There are three theories that offer possible explanations. The first and probably most plausible theory has to do with caffeine's ability to enhance fat utilization for energy. Caffeine stimulates the production of adrenaline, a hormone that accelerates the release of fatty acids into the bloodstream. At the beginning of exercise, the muscles start using these available fatty acids for energy while sparing some of your muscle glycogen.

The second theory goes like this: As a stimulant, caffeine somehow maximizes the force of muscular contractions. But the research here has been conflicting and inconclusive.

The third theory states that caffeine, because of its effect on the central nervous system, might have the psychological effect of making athletes feel they are not working as hard. This theory has been difficult to substantiate, however.

Caffeine Use in Power Sports

Until recently, it was believed that caffeine doesn't help you much if your sports skills relate mainly to strength and power. But Dr. Larry Spriet and his colleagues at the University of Guelph in Ontario might disagree. They have looked into the effect of caffeine on power sports. In one study, 14 exercisers did three bouts of exercise as hard as they could. Each bout was separated by six minutes of rest. The first two exercise bouts lasted two minutes each, and the third bout was performed to exhaustion. The exercisers were tested twice, once with caffeine and once with a placebo. In the third bout, they were able to exercise longer using caffeine (4.93 minutes with caffeine compared to 4.12 minutes with the placebo). Caffeine clearly boosted performance in short-term, intense exercise.

But how? The mechanism is not exactly clear, but the researchers were able to rule out one possibility. By taking blood samples and muscle biopsies, they found that caffeine did not spare muscle glycogen, as was previously thought.

Well-Trained Athletes Do Best

Studies also show that caffeine works best as a power booster if you are well conditioned. Proof of this comes from experiments with swimmers, whose sport is anaerobic as well as aerobic. Highly trained swimmers improved their swimming velocity significantly after consuming 250 milligrams of caffeine, then swimming at maximal speed. Untrained, occasional swimmers didn't fare as well. The same group of researchers had previously conducted experiments with untrained subjects who cycled against resistance after supplementing with caffeine. Again, caffeine did not provide much of a performance boost in untrained individuals.

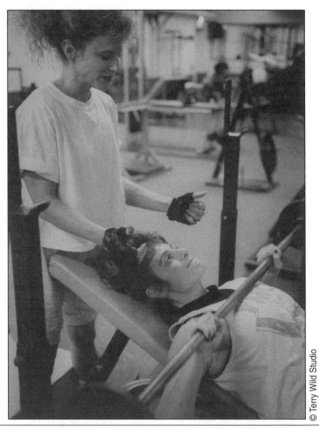

© Terry Wild Studio

If you are well conditioned, caffeine may bolster your workout.

The Final Word

Caffeine does give you a kick for exercise (especially if you're in super shape), though no one has pinpointed exactly why and how. If you want to judge caffeine's effect on your own performance, start off with a little bit—maybe a cup or half a cup of coffee—before your workout. A cup of coffee contains between 108 and 150 milligrams of caffeine. See what happens, and compare it to the workouts when you don't consume caffeine beforehand. Overall, laboratory studies suggest that supplementing with doses of three to six milligrams per kilogram of body weight 30 to 60 minutes before exercise can enhance both power and endurance exercise in well-trained individuals. However, study results in the laboratory might not be the same as results in the real world of the gym.

Keep in mind, too, that caffeine may aggravate certain health problems such as ulcers, heart disease, high blood pressure, and anemia, to name just a few. Stick to your doctor's advice. Above all, don't substitute caffeine for sound, common sense nutritional practices for extending energy.

DIET IS KEY

Building fit, firm muscle—is it as easy as just exercising and supplementing? No, there is a lot more to it than that. You can't neglect a good diet. Refer to the sample strength-training diets in chapter 11. Above all, eat enough quality calories each day to fuel your body for exercise and activity. Then add supplements to further set the muscle-building process in motion.

Sport Nutrition Fact vs. Fiction: Four Supplements That Promise More Than They Produce

The search for ways to improve performance and build strength is as old as athletics itself. Ancient Greeks in the third century ate herbs and mushrooms in an attempt to improve their athletic performance. In the 19th century, European cyclists dipped caffeine-based sugar cubes into nitroglycerin and ate them right before competition. Athletes in bygone eras would also concoct a mixture of coca leaves and wine as an energy stimulant.

Today, the search continues, with new pills and potions appearing all the time, backed by alluring promotions. Here is a look at four of the latest supplements now in the spotlight—and what they can or cannot do for you.

Vanadyl Sulfate

The supplement vanadyl sulfate is a commercial derivative of vanadium, a trace mineral found in vegetables and fish. The body needs very little vanadium, and more than 90 percent of it is excreted in the urine. At high doses, vanadium is extremely toxic and may cause excessive fatigue. To the knowledge of the medical community, no one has ever been diagnosed with a vanadium deficiency disease.

As a supplement, vanadyl sulfate is supposed to have a tissue-building effect by moving glucose and amino acids into the muscles faster and elevating insulin to promote growth. But the evidence for this has been found only in rats. Still, vanadyl sulfate is being aggressively marketed as a tissue-building supplement for strength trainers and athletes.

But does it work the magic it promotes? A group of researchers in New Zealand asked the same question. In a 12-week study, 40 strength trainers (30 men and 10 women) took either a placebo or a daily dose of vanadyl sulfate in amounts matched to their weight (half a milligram per kilogram of body weight). So that strength could be assessed, the strength trainers performed bench presses and leg extensions in 1- and 10-repetition maximum bouts during the course of the experiment.

The findings of the study were that vanadyl sulfate did not increase lean body mass. There were some modest improvements in strength-training performance, but these improvements were short lived, tapering off after the first month of the study. About 20 percent of the strength trainers experienced extreme fatigue during and after training.

In my opinion, there is no reason to supplement with vanadyl sulfate. You can get what it promises with the nutritional methods discussed elsewhere in this chapter.

DHEA

DHEA (dehydroepiandrosterone) is everywhere—pharmacies, grocery stores, health food stores, and department stores. Promoted as an antiaging product, DHEA is probably the most talked about, most hyped supplement on the shelves. Near-magical properties have been attached to DHEA, ranging from increased sex drive to higher energy levels. Bodybuilders, strength trainers, and other athletes take it with the hope that it will build muscle and burn fat.

DHEA is a steroid that is naturally secreted by the adrenal glands. In fact, it is the most abundant steroid in the bloodstream, concentrated mostly in brain tissues. Because DHEA levels decline steadily with age, there is a lot of speculation that it may postpone, even reverse, some of the effects of aging.

When taken as a supplement, DHEA breaks down and is converted to both estrogen and testosterone. The fact that DHEA turns into testosterone, a muscle-building steroid, makes it very appealing to bodybuilders and other athletes who want to build muscle. But there is no real evidence that DHEA supplementation builds muscle. Like all anabolic steroids, DHEA has side effects. Among them are excessive hair growth in women and breast enlargement in men.

A major issue with DHEA is that there have been no long-term human experiments with it. Like most of these overhyped supplements, DHEA has been tested mostly in rats. Extrapolating results from rat studies to humans is just too much of a stretch. Long-term, large-scale, and properly controlled studies are needed on DHEA. At this point, the benefits of DHEA are all speculation. Don't take it, even in small doses. Once you start tinkering with your hormonal system, you are flirting with physiological disaster.

Conjugated Linoleic Acid (CLA)

Derived from safflower oil, CLA is promoted as a fat-burning, muscle-toning, energy-boosting agent. A magazine that was considering running an ad for CLA-containing products sent me the ad for my opinion. I pointed out that the claims regarding reduced body fat and improved muscle tone were not true, unless "in rats" was added to the copy. Once again, a supplement manufacturer took some scant research from a rat study and tried to infer that it would work miracles in humans. This is so misleading. We know zilch about CLA in humans. There is nothing to sell with CLA, except empty hope.

HMB

The supplement HMB, technically known as beta-hydroxy-beta-methylbutyrate, has received a lot of press in bodybuilding magazines, all of it centered on a single study. The study in question showed that HMB increased muscle and decreased body fat in strength-training athletes. The study, which was quoted on the label of the supplement's bottle, wasn't actually published except as an abstract (brief summary). A patent on the product is owned by the university that conducted the study. That represents a potential conflict of interest and makes me question why HMB is being so heavily promoted.

Found in grapefruit, catfish, and other foods, HMB is a breakdown product of the branched-chain amino acid leucine. Your body produces it naturally from proteins containing leucine. Lots of animal studies have been conducted on HMB, and most have shown that supplementation increases lean tissue and enhances the immune system. These findings have prompted the use of HMB as an additive in animal feed.

To date, there has been only one study published in a scientific journal on the effects of HMB supplementation in humans. In the first part of this study, 41 strength trainers were given either 1.5 or 3.0 grams of HMB daily, or none at all, for three weeks. They worked out for one and a half hours three days a week throughout the course of the study. In the second part of the study, the athletes took 3.0 grams of HMB daily or none at all for seven weeks. During the experiment, they worked out for two to three hours a day, six days a week.

HMB supplementation had some effects. In the first part of the study, both dosage levels (1.5 and 3.0 grams) reduced muscle damage brought on by strength training. Compared to the unsupplemented athletes, those on HMB experienced higher strength levels. In the second part of the study, lean mass increased in the HMB-supplemented group, compared to the unsupplemented group.

While these results give promising marks to HMB, a lot more research is needed. You really should not judge a supplement on the basis of a single study.

Table 7.3 provides a quick checklist, rating supplements that are being marketed for strength trainers and which may or may not be worth a try.

TABLE 7.3	Rating Supplements for Strength Trainers		
Supplement	**Definitely worth it**	**Possibly useful**	**Questionable**
Calories	•		
Liquid carb supplements	•		
Carb/protein supplements		•	
Creatine	•		
Creatine with carbs		•	
Weight-gain powders		•	
Carnitine			•
Caffeine		•	
Herbs			•
Vanadyl sulfate			•
DHEA			•
CLA			•
HMB			•

BURNING BODY FAT

Why do you want to lose body fat? To compete in a lower weight class? Get ready for a bodybuilding contest? Improve your performance? Look better in your clothes?

All are admirable goals for fat loss, and there are umpteen ways to reach them. Two of the most widely used, though I don't recommend them, are crash dieting and fad dieting. Crash dieting involves a drastic reduction in calories, usually to about 800 calories or fewer a day, with equally drastic consequences, such as the following:

- Muscle and fluid losses, along with fat loss. If you lost 20 pounds in 20 days, the first six to 10 pounds would be fluid; the rest, fat and muscle. So you are not gaining anything by dropping a lot of weight in a short period of time.

- Loss of aerobic power. Your body's capacity to take in and process oxygen, or $\dot{V}O_2$max, will decline significantly. As a result, less oxygen will be available to help your muscle cells combust fat for fuel.

- Loss of strength. That is a major handicap if you need strength and power for competition—or to get through a workout without fizzling out.

- Metabolic slowdown. Crash dieting slows your metabolic rate down to a crawl. Metabolic rate refers to the speed at which your body processes the food you eat into energy and bodily structures. It is made up of two interrelated factors: basal metabolic rate (BMR) and resting metabolic rate (RMR). Your BMR represents the energy it takes just to exist. Or put another way, your BMR is the energy required to keep your heart beating, your lungs breathing, and your other vital internal functions going strong. Basal metabolic needs must be met. If you're a woman, for example, you spend as many as 1,200 to 1,400 calories a day just to maintain the basic work of your body's cells. Imagine the harm you are doing to life processes by subsisting on an 800-calorie-a-day diet!

Your RMR includes the BMR, plus additional energy expenditures required for activity. Your RMR accounts for about 60 percent of the energy you expend daily. The higher this rate, the more efficient your body is at burning fat.

Specifically, it is your RMR that slows down when you restrict calories. In a one-year study of overweight men, those who cut calories to lose weight (as opposed to those who exercised) experienced a significant drop in their RMR. One reason was that they lost muscle tissue, and RMR is closely linked to how much muscle you have. The moral of the story here is that restrictive diets, if followed for an extended period, will decelerate your RMR and kiss good-bye the muscle you worked so hard to build.

Crash dieting is a losing proposition all the way around. There is nothing to be gained—except more weight! Ninety-five to 99 percent of all people who go on such diets are likely to regain their weight, with interest, within a year.

Fad diets—eating plans that eliminate certain foods and emphasize others—are just as bad. A major problem with fad diets is that they are nutritionally unbalanced, and you could be missing out on some of the key nutrients you need for good health. In fact, an analysis of 11 popular diets revealed deficiencies in one or more essential nutrients, and for several of the B-complex vitamins, calcium, iron, or zinc. One diet derived 70 percent of its calories from fat. Such dangerously high levels of fat can lead to heart disease.

But there are other problems, too. Take the high-protein diet, one of the most popular fad diets among strength trainers. And no wonder it is popular! At first, it works great. You get on the scale, see a huge weight loss, and feel wonderful—until you go off the diet. The weight comes back as fast as it left. That is because high-protein diets are very dehydrating; they flush water right out of your system to help the body get rid of excess nitrogen. Dehydration is dangerous, too, potentially causing fatigue, lack of coordination, heat illnesses such as heat stress and heat stroke, and in extreme cases (a loss of 6 percent or more of body fluid), death. Even with a mere 2 percent drop in body weight as fluid, your performance will diminish. That is the equivalent of three pounds of water loss in a 150 pound person.

Enough said about what doesn't work. There are antifat exercise and diet strategies that do work, namely a fat-burning training program and an individualized, nutritionally balanced eating plan that emphasizes carbohydrates and de-emphasizes fat. Before beginning, set some physique goals.

GO FOR YOUR GOAL

Whether you realize it or not, you already know what your goal is. Just ask yourself: At what weight, or body fat percentage, do I look, feel, or perform the best? The answer to that question is your goal.

The first step is to figure out how close to, or far from, the mark you are.

There are lots of ways to figure this out, including height and weight charts, body mass index (BMI) calculations, and the bathroom scales. But the problem with most of these is that they are not very accurate for people who strength train. None of these methods takes into account the amount of muscle you have on your body. In fact, they might indicate that you are overweight!

Bathroom scales tempt you to step on them every morning. That can be a downer because your weight goes up and down daily as a result of normal fluid fluctuations. You can get very obsessed with the numbers you see on your scales.

A better measurement technique is body-composition testing, which determines how much of your weight is muscle or fat. There are several methods in use. One is underwater weighing, considered to be the gold standard and very accurate if done properly with the right equipment. But it is not very convenient—I certainly don't have a water tank in my office—and it can be rather expensive.

Another method is bioelectrical impedance analysis (BIA), which involves passing a painless electrical current through the body via electrodes placed on the hands and feet. Fat tissue won't conduct the current but fat-free tissue (namely water found in muscle) will. Thus, the faster the current passes through the body, the less body fat there is. Readings obtained from the test are plugged into special formulas adjusted for height, sex, and age to calculate body fat and fat-free mass percentages. The problem with BIA is that your level of hydration dramatically affects the outcome. If you are dehydrated even a little, as most people are, you just won't get an accurate reading. What's more, the equations have not been developed with the muscular, athletic physique in mind.

Among the most accurate of the indirect methods is the skinfold technique, which measures fat just under the skin and uses those measurements to calculate body composition, including body fat percentage. One of the keys to getting accurate and reliable measurements with the skinfold method is to use the same technician, time after time, month after month. That way, you don't get as much variability in the measurements.

I use another strategy with strength trainers and athletes, one that can be a real motivator and reinforcement as you progress toward your goal. Simply use the skinfold caliper device to measure the skinfolds at selected points on your upper arm, chest, waist, hips, thighs, and calves. Do not plug these readings into the equation; instead, record them.

Do this every four to six weeks, being careful to position the calipers at the same site each time you measure a body part. You can even plot your measurements over time as evidence of the positive changes strength training, combined with the right diet, makes in your body.

Your Optimal Body Fat Percentage

Exactly what is optimal in terms of body fat? Healthy ranges of body fat are 22 to 25 percent for women and 15 to 20 percent for men. But if you are a strength trainer or bodybuilder, it is desirable to have even lower percentages: 18 to 10 percent for women and 15 to 7 percent for men.

A lot of elite women athletes, however, have less than 10 percent body fat. Competitive female runners, for example, may have as little as 5 or 6 percent body fat, according to some studies. A low percentage of body fat may be perfectly normal for some women athletes, and desirable because it enhances sports performance. As long as you don't consciously restrict calories while training for a sport, there

Elite female athletes may have less than 10 percent body fat.

is nothing unhealthy about having a naturally lean figure. However, calorie restriction, combined with overexercising, depletes body fat stores to unhealthy levels. This depletion can lead to an estrogen deficiency similar to that which occurs during menopause, and your periods cease. This condition is called amenorrhea. There are some risky side effects to amenorrhea, including premature osteoporosis, heart disease, and the inability to become pregnant.

For women who are not elite athletes, a body fat percentage under 14 can be risky. Hormone levels start to change, and this can lead to the same health problems.

Men are naturally leaner than women are. Even when men and women follow the exact same exercise and diet program, the men will typically lose more body fat. Women usually carry more body fat, since fat provides much of the energy for pregnancy and lactation. A woman's body thus tends to hang onto its fat, which partially explains why it is so hard to get body fat to budge.

If a man's body fat stores dip too low, there could be trouble, too. Strong evidence for this comes from a study of Army Rangers who were put through an eight-week training course involving strenuous exercise and drills. Their food intake was reduced drastically, often to just one meal a day. By the end of the experiment, the soldiers had lost as much as 16 percent of their body weight and had reduced their body fat to 4 to 6 percent. At these low levels, their bodies were starting to feed on muscle tissue for energy. Clearly, the message for men is to not go below 6 percent body fat or you could sacrifice precious muscle mass. Even the leanest athletes I have worked with have never reduced their body fat to less than 4 percent.

How Much Fat Do You Want to Lose?

Once you have determined your body composition through an appropriate method, you can figure out how many pounds you need to lose to reach a lower body fat percentage with the following formula:

1. Present body weight × present body fat % = fat weight

2. Present body weight − fat weight = fat-free weight

3. Fat-free weight/desired % of fat-free mass = goal weight

4. Present body weight − goal weight = weight-loss goal

As an illustration, let's say you presently weigh 140 pounds, with a present body fat percentage of 12 percent. Your goal is to achieve 7 percent body fat. Your goal weight will be composed of 7 percent fat and 93 percent fat-free mass. How many pounds do you need to lose? Here's the calculation:

1. 140 lbs $\times$ .12 = 16.8 lbs fat weight
2. 140 lbs – 16.8 lbs = 123.2 lbs fat-free weight
3. 123.2 lbs / .93 = 132.5 lbs
4. 140 lbs – 132.5 lbs = 7.5 lbs

So, to arrive at 7 percent body fat, you need to lose seven and a half pounds. Naturally, you want those seven plus pounds to be fat pounds. Here's a look at how to maximize your fat loss and minimize your muscle loss.

ANTIFAT EXERCISE STRATEGIES

Your objective is to lose body fat without losing muscle mass. You don't want to lose strength or endurance, either, and you don't want your performance to suffer. So how can you keep on the "losing" track? Forget about diet for a moment; the real key is exercise.

Exercise and Fat Loss

When it comes to burning fat, exercise is your best friend—in three ways:

1.   The more exercise you do, the less you have to worry about calories. One pound of body fat equals 3,500 calories. By burning 250 to 500 calories a day through exercise, you could lose up to a pound of fat a week (7 days $\times$ 500 calories per day = 3,500 calories)—without restricting food. If you need to lose extra body fat, either for competition, health, appearance, or performance, the solution may be as simple as increasing your activity. During an intense strength-training program, for example, you can expend as many as 500 calories an hour; walking at a brisk pace burns 300 calories an hour; bicycling, 600 calories an hour; or aerobic dancing, up to 500 calories an hour.

2.   Exercise hikes your resting metabolic rate. After you exercise, your resting metabolic rate stays elevated for several hours, and you

burn extra calories even at rest. And if you strength train, you get even more of a metabolic boost: The muscle you develop is calorie-burning, metabolically active tissue. Having more of muscle tissue cranks your metabolic rate up even higher. In fact, muscle requires roughly 45 calories a day to function, even at rest.

At Colorado State University, researchers recruited 10 men, ages 22 to 35, to see what effect, if any, strength training had on metabolism. At various times in the study, the men participated in strength training, aerobic exercise, or a control condition of quiet sitting. During the experiment, the subjects were fed controlled diets with a composition of 65 percent carbohydrate, 15 percent protein, and 20 percent fat.

In the strength-training portion of the experiment, the men performed a fairly standard yet strenuous routine: five sets of 10 different upper and lower body exercises for a total of 50 sets. They worked out for about 100 minutes. For aerobic exercise, the men cycled at moderate intensities for about an hour.

The researchers reported these findings: Strength training produced a higher rate of oxygen usage than either aerobic exercise or quiet sitting, meaning that it was a better elevator of resting metabolic rate. In fact, the men's RMR stayed elevated for about 15 hours after working out. Clearly, strength training stood out as a metabolic booster and a calorie burner. With strength training, it is easy to keep fat off and control your weight.

3. Exercise preserves muscle. If you lose 10 pounds of body weight, you may be lighter, but if five of those pounds are muscle, you sure won't be stronger, and your performance can really suffer. Appearance-wise, you can still look flabby when muscle tissue is lost. Exercise is one of the best ways to make sure you are shedding weight from fat stores, rather than from muscle stores.

Researchers have put this principle to the test. In a study of 10 overweight women, half of the women were placed in a diet-plus-exercise group and half of the women in an exercise-only group. The women in the diet-plus-exercise group followed a diet that reduced their calories by 50 percent of what it took to maintain their weight. They worked out aerobically six times a week. The exercise-only group followed the same aerobic exercise program but followed a diet designed to stabilize their weight.

After 14 weeks, it was time to check the results. Here is what happened: Both groups lost weight. But the composition of that loss was vastly different between the groups. In the diet-plus-exercise group, the weight lost was 67 percent fat and 33 percent lean mass.

In the exercise-only group, the women lost much more fat—86 percent fat and only 14 percent lean mass! Not only that, RMR declined by 9 percent among the dieters, whereas it was maintained in the exercisers.

What does all this tell us? Sure, you can lose weight by low-calorie dieting. But you risk losing muscle. Not only that, your metabolic rate can plummet, sabotaging your attempts at successful weight control. With exercise and a nonrestrictive diet, you preserve calorie-burning muscle and keep your metabolism in gear.

Exercise Intensity Counts

"Intensity" has several different meanings depending on the type of exercise you do, but it basically describes how hard you work out. With aerobic exercise, intensity can be measured by heart rate, which indicates the amount of work your heart does to keep up with the demands of various activities, including exercise.

For optimum fat burning, you should exercise at a level hard enough to raise your heart rate to 70 to 85 percent or higher of your maximum heart rate, which is expressed as 220 minus your age. At low-intensity exercise—20 minutes or longer at around 50 percent of your maximum heart rate—fat supplies as much as 90 percent of your fuel requirements.

Higher intensity aerobic exercise at roughly 75 percent of your maximum heart rate burns a smaller percentage of fat (around 60 percent), but results in more total calories burned overall, including more fat calories.

To illustrate this concept, here's a comparison based on studies of aerobic intensity. At 50 percent of your maximum heart rate, you burn 7 calories a minute, 90 percent of which come from fat. At 75 percent of your maximum heart rate, you burn 14 calories a minute, 60 percent from fat. So at 50 percent intensity, where 90 percent of the calories are from fat, you are burning only 6.30 fat calories per minute (0.90 × 7 calories/minute), but at 75 percent intensity, where only 60 percent of the calories are from fat, you are burning as much as 8.40 fat calories per minute (0.60 × 14 calories/minute). In short, you burn more total fat calories at higher intensities.

If it is difficult for you to exercise at a high intensity, try increasing your duration—how long you exercise. You can burn just as much fat at a lower intensity by working out longer as you can by exercising at a higher intensity.

To increase your rate of fat loss, gradually increase your aerobic exercise sessions from 30 to 60 minutes or strive for longer distances. For example, jogging a mile expends about 100 calories. Jog five miles, and you will burn 500 calories. If you are jogging only a mile a day, it would take a month to lose a pound of fat, compared to about a week if you jog five miles a day.

Another option related to duration is frequency—working out more times a week to obtain a greater caloric expenditure. Perhaps you could add bicycling or aerobic dance to your aerobics program for some variety, as well as for some extra calorie burning.

Intensity in strength training refers to how much weight you lift. For your muscles to respond—that is, get stronger and better developed—you have to challenge them to handle heavier poundages. That means continually putting more demands on them than they're used to; in other words, progressively increasing your poundages from workout to workout. The more muscle you can develop, the more efficient your body becomes at fat burning, since muscle is the most metabolically active tissue in the body.

The Competitive Strategy of a Professional Bodybuilder

Several years ago, a group of researchers at Arizona State University studied the diet and exercise strategies of Mike Ashley, known in bodybuilding circles as "the Natural Wonder" because he does not use anabolic steroids. During an eight-week precontest period, Mike did the following:

• Consumed roughly 5,000 calories daily—3,674 calories from food, plus a carbohydrate-rich sport drink, and an amino acid supplement.

• Supplemented with an additional 1,278 calories a day from supplemental MCT oil. (This meant that 25.5 percent of his calories came from a fat source, not including food intake. However, MCTs are not metabolized like conventional fats; the body uses them immediately for energy, rather than storing them as fat. While MCTs represent a more compact source of energy (nine calories per gram versus four calories per gram for carbs), this approach is not recommended for everyone. The nutrition plan outlined in chapter 11 has wider application and will work for more people.)

• Trained on a stair-climbing machine for a full hour, six days a week.

• Weight trained six days a week, dividing his routine into two or three workouts a day. In total, Mike worked out five to six hours a day at a very high level of intensity.

With these strategies—lots of quality calories and lots of intense exercise—Mike was able to reduce his body fat from 9 percent to a contest-sharp 6.9 percent, without sacrificing muscle.

You don't have to start working out five hours a day (unless perhaps you are a professional bodybuilder training for a contest). But there is a connection between exercise and diet to burn body fat. You don't necessarily have to cut calories. In fact, you can keep them high. Exercising at moderate to high levels of intensity will take care of the fat.

ANTIFAT DIET STRATEGIES

Here's how to eat to give yourself the best chances at losing fat and saving muscle.

1.   Don't fast. Because you strength train and probably do aerobics as well, you actually need more food, not less. Researchers at Tufts University found that when older men and women began a strength-training program, they needed 15 percent more calories just to maintain their body weight. This finding is not so surprising, really. With strength training, the exercisers began to expend more calories. Plus, their resting metabolic rate increased because they had built more muscle.

You can figure out exactly how many calories you personally need to lose fat. Based on my research with competitive bodybuilders, I have concluded that an intake of 35 to 38 calories per kilogram of body weight a day is reasonable for fat loss and muscle preservation. The minimum is 30 to 33 calories per kilogram for a rapid cut. Anything under that is too restrictive, and you won't be well nourished.

Let's say you weigh 180 pounds (82 kilograms). Here's how to figure your calorie requirements to lose fat: 82 kilograms × 35 calories/kilogram = 2,870 calories. For maintaining body weight, you should eat up to 44 calories per kilogram of body weight a day, or 3,608 calories a day. If you increase your exercise intensity, duration, or frequency, go even higher—to 54 calories per kilogram of body weight, or 4,428 calories a day.

If you still need a calorie deficit to continue losing fat or to break a plateau, get that deficit by increasing your activity level and modifying your calories slightly. For example, restrict your calories by about 500 a day and increase aerobic exercise—maybe by 500 calories a day. That way, you would have an energy deficit of 1,000 calories.

2.   Slash the fat. Fat calories are more likely to be deposited as body fat. The reason has to do with the thermic effect of food, which describes the energy spent to metabolize food. Very little energy is expended to metabolize fat compared to carbohydrates. The energy cost of metabolizing carbs and converting them to glycogen for storage is rated at 25 percent, in contrast to just 4 percent to store fat. In other words, your body works harder at breaking down carbs and using them for energy. This is not so with fat. The body recognizes fat as fat and prefers to hang on to it, rather than break it down for energy. As noted in chapter 4, your fat intake should be 20 percent or less of your total daily calories.

3.   Preserve muscle with protein. To lose mostly fat, with muscle mass preserved, you must have adequate protein in your diet. If you go on a diet that is too low in calories, there is a good chance that your dietary protein would not be used to build tissue but instead might be broken down and used for energy much like carbs and fat are.

So how much protein do you need to maximize muscle mass while minimizing body fat? Those of us who work with strength-training athletes favor eating 1.6 grams of protein per kilogram of body weight. In a study of 19 drug-free bodybuilders, researchers at Virginia Tech divided the athletes into three groups: a high-protein/moderate-carbohydrate group, a moderate-protein/high-carbohydrate group, and a control group. The high-protein/moderate-carb group consumed twice the RDA for protein, or 1.6 grams per kilogram of body weight, while the moderate-protein/high-carbohydrate group consumed the RDA (0.8 grams per kilogram of body weight).

With the high-protein/moderate-carbohydrate diet, more body protein was retained than with the other diet, which meant that the extra protein was being used to synthesize and repair new tissue. One drawback of the higher-protein diet, however, was that it compromised muscular endurance, the ability to repeat contractions over and over without fatiguing. Even so, the overall results of this study suggest that if you are trying to lose body fat, you should eat more than the RDA of protein to protect your muscle mass. But keep your carbs up too, so you can maintain high levels of exercise intensity.

4.   Concentrate on carbs. Regardless of what you hear or read, carbohydrates are critical to fat loss for reasons that bear repeating. First, carbohydrates are required in the cellular reactions involved in burning fat.

Second, they spare protein from being used as fuel. Your body prefers to burn carbohydrates for energy over protein. Protein is thus spared so that it can be used to do its main job of repairing tissue and building lean muscle.

© Mary Langenfeld

A reduction in body fat may improve athletic performance.

Third, carbohydrates restock the body with glycogen, which helps power the muscles during exercise. The more glycogen in the muscles, the harder you can train. Hard training burns body fat and builds metabolically active muscle.

Fourth, when your body is digesting carbohydrates, your metabolic rate goes up higher than it does when metabolizing fat. This is due to the thermic effect of food—the energy cost of assimilating food.

Finally, carbohydrates (namely, complex carbs) are loaded with fiber, which has its own set of fat-burning benefits. More energy (calories) is spent digesting and absorbing high-fiber foods than most foods. Fiber keeps your appetite in check by stimulating the release of appetite-suppressing hormones. Additionally, fiber accelerates the time it takes for food to move through your body, meaning fewer calories are left to be stored as fat. So you see: Carbs are key for fat burning.

If you are strength training and doing aerobics as part of your fat-loss program, you need to eat 8 to 10 grams of carbohydrate per kilogram of body weight daily. That amount will keep you well fueled for high-intensity exercise.

5.   Cut down on sugary foods. One type of carb to go easy on is sugar, and foods that contain a lot of it. Sugar-laced foods have a fattening effect on the body. The reason is that many sugary foods, particularly dessert-type foods such as ice cream, cakes, and pies, contain a lot of fat. Overindulging in these foods increases your risk of gaining body fat.

Researchers at Indiana University in Bloomington, Indiana, analyzed the diets of four groups of people: lean men (average body fat was 15 percent), lean women (average body fat was 20 percent), obese men (average body fat was 25 percent), and obese women (average body fat was 35 percent).

The obese men and women ate more of their calories from fat (as high as 36 percent of total calories) and refined sugars such as candy, doughnuts, and ice cream, which are also high in fat, than the lean men and women. In other words, there was a link between high-fat, high-sugar diets and obesity.

The lesson here is: Change the composition of your diet to keep the fat off. This means cutting down on high-fat sugary foods. The easiest way to do this is by increasing the complex carbs in your diet. Remember, 70 percent of your total daily calories should come from carbs.

If you have a sweet tooth, you may want to choose sweets that are primarily carbohydrate and not fat. Even so, don't overindulge on these either, since they are not as nutrient dense as complex carbs.

You may have thought about using artificially sweetened foods. But proceed with caution. See the sidebar article for an update on the current controversy over artificial sweeteners.

Do Artificial Sweeteners Have a Place in a Fat Loss Program?

Artificial sweeteners are swirling in controversy. As a strength trainer, be aware of the controversies because you most likely eat a lot of food—some of which you may sweeten with these products.

The oldest artificial sweetener on the market is saccharin. A zero-calorie sweetener, saccharin was originally developed in 1900 to help diabetics and improve the taste of other medically supervised diets. Nearly 100 years later, the use of artificial sweeteners has become enormously popular, and there are several new products to choose from (see table 8.1).

Cyclamate, also a noncalorie sweetener, was introduced in the 1950s. It tasted better than saccharin and soon surpassed it in popularity. However, in the 1970s, the FDA banned its use in foods after studies showed that it increased the risk of cancer in animals. Then in 1977, because of research suggesting that saccharin caused bladder tumors in rats, the FDA required a warning label on all saccharin-containing foods.

In 1981, the FDA approved the use of a new artificial sweetener, aspartame. Commercially available as Equal, aspartame is an artificially synthesized compound of two natural ingredients, the amino acids phenylalanine and aspartic acid. Aspartame is virtually calorie free and 200 times sweeter than sugar.

Aspartame's natural ingredients and superior taste catapulted it to popularity. But no sooner had the FDA approved the use of aspartame, than its apparent safety came into question.

It was already well known that eating aspartame could be dangerous for people with phenylketonuria (PKU), an inability to metabolize phenylalanine. All products containing aspartame must be labeled with a warning for individuals who have PKU. But the specter of other risks to normal, healthy people began to rise among the scientific community.

According to researchers, there may be populations other than those with PKU that are sensitive to aspartame. Mood-disorder patients are one example. A study conducted at Northeastern Ohio University's College of Medicine had to be halted because a group of patients with clinical depression had severe reactions to aspartame.

The question of whether aspartame could cause brain tumors in rats was a focus of research reviews and discussions conducted by the FDA prior to approving the sweetener. Now some researchers are claiming that there were flaws in the FDA's research and review process regarding the risk of brain tumors.

To date, the FDA stands by its approval. However, Dr. John Olney, a neuroscientist at the Washington University School of Medicine, disagrees with the decision. After studying aspartame's effects on the brain for more than 20 years, Dr. Olney feels that there may be a link between the rising rates of brain tumors in the United States and the nearly 17 years of aspartame use in foods. According to Dr. Olney, "About three to five years after aspartame was approved, there's been a striking increase in the incidence of malignant brain tumors."

Dr. Olney is not calling for a ban on aspartame. In an interview, he stated: "I'm not saying that aspartame has been proven to cause brain tumors. I'm saying that there is enough basis to suspect aspartame, that it needs to be reassessed."

As long as the safety of these products remains in question, I recommend that you use them in moderation, if at all.

6. Don't skip breakfast. Skipping breakfast is not a good way to lose body fat. In fact, it could fatten you up! Most people who skip breakfast make up those calories, with interest, throughout the day. In Madrid, Spain, researchers found that overweight and obese people spent less time eating breakfast, and ate smaller quantities and less varied types of food at breakfast compared to normal-weight people.

Eating breakfast stokes your metabolic fires for the day. By contrast, going hungry in the morning is just another form of fasting,

TABLE 8.1	Fake Sugars	
Brand name	**Calories/serving**	**Advantages/disadvantages**
Saccharin	4	Bitter aftertaste; has been found to cause cancer in lab rats.
Aspartame	4	Good taste; destroyed during cooking; may cause reactions in vulnerable populations.
Acesulfame-K	0	As sweet as aspartame but more stable and less expensive; consumer safety groups concerned about safety.
Cyclamate	0	Lacks FDA approval; has been linked to cancer in lab rats.

which slows down your metabolism. Plus, your physical and mental performance will suffer when you are running on empty.

If you are like me, you're rushed in the morning, with barely enough time to shower and dress, let alone eat breakfast. If that is the case, eat what you can. Something is better than nothing. A study done in England found that because ready-to-eat cereals are high in vitamins and minerals and low in fat, they make a great choice for breakfast.

The best breakfasts include a combination of carbohydrate, protein, and fat. They should meet about one-quarter to one-third of your daily caloric requirements. If you live an on-the-go lifestyle, you need some nutritious breakfasts that take minutes to fix. There are several breakfast recipes in chapter 11 to help you. Some of these can even go on the road with you—so there is no excuse to skip breakfast again!

INDIVIDUALIZE YOUR DIET

Making dietary changes doesn't mean giving up your favorite foods or altering your lifestyle. Simply moderate how much of your favorite foods you eat by having them less often, and then learn how to make healthier substitutions.

Take the case of Doug, a 17-year-old defensive lineman. His dream was to play quarterback. But he just didn't have the speed and was always exhausted by the fourth quarter. After Doug had his body composition tested, his coaches decided that he needed to lose fat.

I analyzed his diet to see where substitutions could be made so that Doug could shed body fat. His breakfast was usually a Danish and orange juice. He replaced the Danish with a more nutritious English muffin.

Doug's typical lunch was a Quarter Pounder with Cheese, french fries, and apple pie. So instead of going to his favorite fast food restaurant, he began eating lunch at the deli next door, where he could order a lower fat meal like chicken on rye and pretzels.

Snacks were usually a cola and a candy bar, high-fat, high-sugary foods that made him feel full and sluggish. Doug switched to a banana instead.

After practice, Doug would have a home-cooked meal for dinner. Here, he substituted a baked potato for mashed potatoes, used a lower fat salad dressing on his salad, and ate low-fat ice milk instead of ice cream for dessert.

These minor alterations resulted in some major changes. Doug's carb intake went up, while his fat intake went down. He was able to trim down without sacrificing muscle. Equally important, he improved his performance on the field. You can achieve the same success by taking a similar approach to dietary planning. Are you game? Then be sure to check out my sample diets in chapter 11 for examples of how to eat to lose fat.

Sport Nutrition Fact vs. Fiction: Diet Pills: A Shortcut to Cutting Up?

Should you use diet pills to lose fat and make weight? Unequivocally, no.

The latest generation of diet pills includes the appetite suppressants fenfluramine, phentermine, and dexfenfluramine (Redux). These drugs affect chemicals in the brain that short-circuit the desire to eat. The FDA withdrew fenfluramine and Redux from the market in September 1997 after studies found that 30 percent of 290 patients who took them showed signs of heart-valve abnormalities.

Dexfenfluramine has a rare but potentially fatal side effect: primary pulmonary hypertension, in which the blood vessels supplying the lungs become scarred and thickened. The disease is progressive, eventually ending in death within a few years.

Phentermine can still be prescribed. Side effects include dry mouth, nervousness, constipation, and insomnia.

These drugs have been prescribed primarily for people who are considered obese, defined as being at least 20 percent over ideal weight. No ethical physician would recommend or prescribe them for anyone 10 pounds or less over a healthy weight.

What about over-the-counter diet pills? These pills are classified as appetite suppressants, too. They all contain an amphetamine derivative called phenylpropanolamine. A mild stimulant, this drug causes various untoward reactions, including nervousness, anxiety, and increased blood pressure. More troubling is that some people, especially teenagers, can suffer stroke if they exceed the recommended dosage.

Forget diet pills. As a strength trainer, you have the best weapons available to fight body fat: high-energy eating habits and exercise that builds calorie-burning muscle and stokes your metabolic fires.

PEAKING FOR COMPETITION

Perhaps you have decided to take your strength training up a notch to competitive bodybuilding, powerlifting, or weightlifting. Or perhaps you are already a competitive strength trainer who is searching for that extra edge. No matter what your ambition, proper nutrition is the key.

In bodybuilding, you are judged on muscularity (degree of muscular bulk), definition (absence of body fat), symmetry (shape and size of your muscles in proportion to each other), and posing ability. In preparing for competition, you strive to reduce body fat, but without sacrificing muscle mass, to reveal as much muscular definition as possible. In some competitions, bodybuilders compete according to weight classes and are thus concerned about making weight. Bodybuilders typically follow precontest diets to get cut or ripped and to qualify for their weight class.

Unlike bodybuilding competitions, which are judged mostly on appearance, powerlifting or weightlifting meets are judged on strength performance. Your goal is to lift as much weight as possible in various events. Prior to the meet, you are also required to make weight to qualify for a specific weight class. Like a bodybuilder, you must focus on gaining and preserving muscular weight, as well as on losing body fat to achieve your contest weight. Diet therefore plays a critical role in precontest preparation for all competitive strength trainers who want to achieve peak shape.

Until quite recently, most strength athletes partitioned their precontest diets into two distinct phases: a bulking phase, in which the competitor eats huge amounts of food without much regard to fat content or other sound nutrition practices; and a cutting phase, where drastic measures such as starvation-type dieting and drugs are used to lose weight rapidly in the weeks before a contest. Unless sound nutritional practices are followed, the cutting phase can be unhealthy, rigid, monotonous, and risky to performance. The bulking phase tends to pile on fat pounds, which are that much harder to lose when it comes time to prepare for competition.

Today, though, more strength athletes choose to stay in competition shape year round. That way, it is easier to lose body fat because there is less to lose, and the process of cutting up is much safer and more successful.

This chapter discusses a step-by-step precontest diet strategy called tapering that lets you lose maximum body fat, retain hard-earned muscle, and perform at your very best level. This strategy applies mostly to bodybuilders, although other strength athletes can adapt many of the same recommendations. The end of the chapter covers key issues for powerlifters and weightlifters.

STEP 1: PLAN YOUR START DATE

The length of time you spend dieting for a competition depends on how out of shape you are to begin with. If you have let yourself get too fat by bulking up in the off-season, then you will really have to stretch your precontest dieting out by several months.

Don't start your precontest dieting too close to your contest. You will be too tempted to resort to crash dieting. This can result in loss of muscle, decreased strength and power, low energy, moodiness or irritability, and low immunity. Losing lots of fat in a short period of time is virtually impossible for most people, anyway. Physiologically, no one can lose more than four pounds of fat a week, even by total fasting. Take a gradual approach to precontest dieting.

Start your contest preparation about 10 to 12 weeks before your competition. During this period, make slight adjustments in your calorie and nutrient intake, as well as in your aerobic exercise level. Additionally, supplement with creatine and take a carbohydrate/protein supplement immediately following your training session, as suggested in chapter 7.

STEP 2: FIGURE OUT A SAFE LEVEL OF CALORIE REDUCTION

Getting cut is absolutely essential to competitive success in bodybuilding. One way to begin this process is by slightly reducing your caloric intake. By consuming fewer calories, you can gradually reduce body fat to lower levels. But you don't want to cut calories too much. A drastic reduction in calories will downshift your resting metabolic rate (RMR) for two reasons. The first has to do with the thermic effect of food, which is the increase in your RMR after you eat a meal as food is digested and metabolized. Eating more calories increases the thermic effect of food and along with it, the RMR. Likewise, cutting calories decreases the thermic effect of food, as well as the RMR. Without enough calories to drive your metabolic processes, it becomes harder for your body to burn calories to lose body fat.

Second, long periods of calorie deprivation—that is, diets under 1,200 calories a day—lower your RMR as a result of something called the starvation adaptation response. This simply means that your metabolism has slowed down to accommodate your lower caloric intake. Your body is stockpiling dietary fat and calories rather than burning them for energy. You can actually gain body fat on a diet of 1,200 calories or less a day.

The starvation adaptation response has been observed frequently in undernourished endurance athletes. In a study of triathletes, researchers found these athletes weren't consuming enough calories to fuel themselves for training and competition. When calories were increased, the athletes' weight stayed the same. This occurred because their resting metabolic rates returned to normal with the introduction of ample calories. So to keep your metabolism running in high gear, you have to eat enough calories to match your energy requirements.

During pre-contest preparation, reduce your calories by 500 each day. A reduction like this won't adversely affect your resting metabolic rate. At the same time, increase your aerobic exercise to burn 500 calories a day. The two adjustments should allow for an energy deficit of 1,000 calories a day. A pound of fat is equal to 3,500 calories, so with a deficit of 1,000 calories, you should lose one to two pounds of body fat a week—a safe rate of fat loss that should successfully help you get tapered and cut by competition day.

You may want to reduce your caloric intake by only 250 calories, depending on how much fat you need to lose in the allotted time and how efficiently your body burns fat. Here's a suggestion: Try tapering during a noncompetition period to help you get a feel for how much fat your body can actually burn.

Another way to figure out how many calories you need in order to lose body fat is the method of calculating the calories per kilogram of body weight per day. As noted in chapter 8, you generally need about 44 calories or higher per kilogram of body weight a day to maintain your weight (up to 50 to 60 calories per kilogram of body weight a day if your training program includes aerobic exercise). To lose body fat, drop down to 30 to 35 calories per kilogram of body weight a day. Don't go any lower than that, however, because you risk losing muscle.

You might wonder: Why can't I just crash diet for a few weeks to get in shape for my contest? After all, I'm training hard with weights. Shouldn't strength training protect me from losing muscle?

As logical as the argument sounds, scientific research proves otherwise. In one study, overweight women were divided into two groups: a diet-only group or a diet-plus-strength-training group. The experimental diet provided only 800 calories a day, and the study lasted four weeks. Now, the intriguing news: Every woman in both groups lost roughly the same amount of weight (11 pounds). Even the composition of the lost weight was the same. All the women lost eight pounds of fat and three pounds of muscle. The bottom line is that even strength training didn't preserve muscle under low-calorie dieting conditions.

The implications for bodybuilders are clear. In just four short weeks, you can lose precious muscle if you crash diet prior to your contest. Watch how low you go, calorie-wise. Research with body-builders confirms that you can lose muscle in just seven days on calories as low as 18 per kilogram of body weight a day.

STEP 3: INCREASE YOUR AEROBIC EXERCISE

To sculpt a winning physique, increase the intensity and duration of aerobic exercise during your contest preparation phase. Aerobic exercise stimulates the activity of a fat-burning enzyme, technically known as hormone sensitive lipase, which breaks down stored fat and moves it into circulation to be burned for energy. Aerobic exercise also increases $\dot{V}O_2$max, the capability to process oxygen and transport it to body tissues. Fat is burned most efficiently when there is sufficient oxygen available.

If you put a lot of effort into your aerobics, you may not have to reduce your calories. That's the conclusion of a recent study from West Virginia University. Women of normal weight were able to decrease their body fat within three months simply by exercising aerobically four days a week for about 45 minutes each time at a heart rate of between 80 to 90 percent of their maximum. They didn't have to cut calories, yet they still lost plenty of body fat.

© Terry Wild Studio

Intense aerobic exercise is vital during the contest preparation phase.

Here's some good news for aerobically fit bodybuilders. The better trained you are aerobically—and the leaner you are—the better your body can burn fat for energy. By increasing $\dot{V}O_2$max and thus increasing available oxygen to tissues, aerobic exercise enhances the ability of your muscles to combust fat as fuel. At the cellular level, the breakdown of fat speeds up, and it is released faster from storage sites in fat and muscle tissue.

There is no doubt about it: Aerobic exercise is a miracle worker when it comes to fat burning. Stay aerobically fit and lean year round, and you'll have no trouble shedding those last few parcels of pudge prior to contest time.

STEP 4: EAT MORE PROTEIN

During precontest preparation, you should be eating at least 1.8 to 2.0 grams of protein per kilogram of body weight a day. This level will help you maintain muscle mass. Increasing your protein intake during a time of calorie reduction helps protect against muscle loss.

The extra protein can be used as a backup energy source in case your body needs it.

STEP 5: TIME MEALS AND EXERCISE FOR GREATER FAT BURNING

Do you want to maximize fat burning during aerobic exercise? Then don't eat a high-carb meal (especially one that contains high-glycemic foods) within four hours of exercising. This recommendation is the exact opposite of what I would tell an endurance athlete, or a strength trainer during the regular training period. But read on.

Pre-workout carbs curtail your fat-burning ability during the first 50 minutes of moderate-intensity exercise. What happens is this: Carbs trigger the release of insulin into the bloodstream. Insulin keeps the fat-burning enzyme, hormone sensitive lipase, from breaking down stored fat for energy. In the absence of carbs, your body is thus more likely to draw on its fat reserves for energy. You can get leaner as a result.

Eat a little protein in the pre-workout period, instead of carbs, if your body needs some extra nutrient energy. Protein does not inhibit the fat-breakdown process during exercise like carbohydrate does. However, eliminating pre-workout carbs is a practice that should be followed only during your precontest training period.

STEP 6: DON'T NEGLECT CARBS

As far as the rest of your diet is concerned, don't cut your carbs too much, or you are going to be really sluggish. You won't have much charisma on contest day, since a carb-needy body adversely affects your mood. And you could get the shakes when you strike your poses. Clearly, it is critical to have some carbohydrates in your diet throughout the tapering phase.

With the recommended increase in your protein intake, your total calories might look something like this: protein, 20 to 25 percent; carbohydrate, 65 percent; and fat, 10 to 15 percent. As long as you do not cut calories too drastically, you will still have enough carbs to support your training requirements.

STEP 7: LOWER YOUR FAT INTAKE

Watch your fat intake, too. As I explained in chapter 4, fat in the diet turns into fat on the body more easily than carbohydrate does. Thus, it becomes even more critical to avoid high-fat foods during your tapering phase. Make foods like whole grains, pastas, beans, vegetables, and fruits the mainstays of your precontest diet, and you will automatically eat a low-fat diet. This low-fat diet should contain much more unsaturated than saturated fat. See chapter 4 for how to calculate the fat content in your diet.

STEP 8: SPACE YOUR MEALS THROUGHOUT THE DAY

Your body will better use its calories for energy, rather than deposit them as fat, if you eat several small meals throughout the day. Most bodybuilders and other strength athletes eat five, six, or more meals a day. Spacing meals in this manner keeps you well fueled throughout the day. Plus, the more times you eat, the higher your metabolism stays—thanks to the thermic effect of food. In other words, every time you eat, your metabolism accelerates. For best results, don't consume more than 400 to 500 calories at one sitting. Eating multiple meals throughout the day is a good dietary practice to follow, whether or not you are dieting for competition.

STEP 9: SUPPLEMENT PRUDENTLY DURING PRE-CONTEST DIETING AND TRAINING

There are some real nutritional horror stories among bodybuilders, especially women, who diet stringently for contests and then suffer

deficiencies in calcium, magnesium, zinc, vitamin D, and other nutrients. Generally, harmful deficiencies occur because bodybuilders tend
to eliminate dairy foods and red meat during precontest dieting. You
really don't need to shy away from these foods, however. Red meat
can be included in your diet as long as it is lean and cooked appropri-
ately. Nonfat dairy foods, an important source of body-strengthen-
ing minerals, can be included in your diet, too. Neither of these foods
will make you gain fat, as long as you eat them in moderation.

Because calories are cut during precontest diets and some bodybuilders may be on these diets several times a year, supplement with
an antioxidant vitamin/mineral formula that contains 100 percent of
the RDA for all essential nutrients. This type of supplement will help
cover your nutritional bases. See chapter 10 for additional supplement recommendations.

STEP 10: WATCH YOUR WATER INTAKE

Competitive bodybuilders live in dread of water retention, medically known as edema. True, water retention can keep you from
looking cut even after you have pared down to physique perfection.
Water can swell up in certain areas, and you look "fat" even though
it's only water weight.

How can you prevent water retention? Ironically, the best defense
is to drink plenty of water throughout your tapering period. This
means drinking between 8 and 10 glasses, or more, of pure water
daily. With ample fluid, your body automatically flushes itself of
extra water.

Conversely, not drinking enough water can make your body cling
to as much fluid as it can, and you'll end up bloated. Dehydration can
sap your energy, too. If you are low on fluids, you won't be able to
work out as intensely.

Besides drinking plenty of water, try the following strategies to
prevent water retention.

Moderate Your Sodium Intake if You Are Sodium Sensitive

An essential element in our diets, sodium has gained a very bad
reputation among bodybuilders and other athletes trying to make

POWER PROFILES

After breaking his foot, the team captain of a professional football team asked me what he could do nutritionally to help it heal faster. I told him to make sure he was drinking plenty of milk because the calcium in milk would help put his injury on the mend. The problem was, he wasn't a milk drinker due to something called lactose intolerance, a very common food sensitivity.

People with lactose intolerance lack sufficient lactase, the enzyme required to digest lactose, a sugar in milk that helps you absorb calcium from the intestine. About 70 percent of the world's population are lactose-intolerant. The condition causes a range of intestinal disturbances ranging from gas to severe pain and diarrhea.

For anyone with lactose intolerance, there are several options to ensure adequate intake of calcium from milk and milk products. One option is to try drinking small portions of milk at first (one-half cup at a time) to see if this amount can be tolerated. Also, aged cheeses and yogurts with active cultures may be better digested than straight milk.

Products such as enzyme-treated Lactaid milk, or Lactaid enzyme tablets for use at home or on the road, make milk consumption possible. Another enzyme product, Dairyease, is a tablet that, when taken before meals, assists with lactose digestion and lets you drink milk. Upon my suggestion, the football player tried these products and had no problems drinking milk from then on.

weight. Our bodies have a minimum requirement of 500 milligrams per day. The body tightly regulates its electrolyte levels, including sodium. Decreasing sodium levels really doesn't have much of an effect. Your body holds on to the exact amount of sodium it needs, even if you reduce your intake. It is essential to consume the minimum requirement to maintain fluid balance and electrolyte balance. Otherwise, nerve and muscle function will be impaired, and exercise performance will definitely diminish. Some bodybuilders have passed out just before their competition due to dehydration and possible electrolyte imbalance.

If you are sodium sensitive—that is, sodium does cause you to retain water—you probably should reduce your intake slightly. Don't go to extremes, though. Simply avoid high-sodium foods, such as snack foods, canned foods, salted foods, pickled foods, cured foods, and lunch meats. Certainly don't add any extra salt to your food; this is the key. But eliminating natural, whole foods due to their sodium content is usually unnecessary. For instance, most body-builders eliminate all dairy products from their diets during the precompetition phase. Cheese is higher in sodium, but one eight-ounce glass of nonfat milk contains only 126 grams of sodium. Two egg whites, most bodybuilders' favorite source of protein, contain 212 grams of sodium! Milk is also a great source of protein, vitamins, and minerals. So don't let worries about sodium make you eliminate such an important nonfat source of nutrients in your diet. To main-tain a low-sodium diet, concentrate your food choices on whole grains, fresh fruits and vegetables, nonfat dairy foods, and unproc-essed meats.

Diuretics flush sodium and other electrolytes from your body, causing life-threatening imbalances. Avoid diuretics at all cost. And stay away from illegal drugs. Their use is unethical and unhealthy. The healthier you are going into competition, the more likely you are to win.

Eat Vegetables That Are Naturally Diuretic

Some foods naturally help the body eliminate water. These include asparagus, cucumbers, and watercress. You might try eating these on your precontest diet, especially the day before your weigh-in, if water retention is a concern.

Don't Let Up on Your Aerobics

Aerobic exercise improves the resiliency and tone of blood vessels. Unless blood vessels are resilient, water can seep from them and collect in the tissues. Water retention is the result. A regular program of aerobics helps prevent this.

THE WEEK PRIOR TO YOUR COMPETITION

To get supercut competition day, tweak your diet somewhat to chisel away some extra body fat. Cut your calories to 30 calories per kilogram of body weight a day for women, or 33 calories per kilogram of body weight a day for men. Use this approach only when absolutely necessary.

Many strength athletes worry about being too full just as they go into competition. But it is critical to have enough fluid, calories, and nutrients to feel strong and look great. Probably the best way to do this is to use liquid meal-replacement supplements. These will charge you up, but pass through your digestive system more quickly than solid foods. Because each serving is about the calorie level of a small meal or snack, you should drink one serving, two and a half to three hours before your competition. If you feel comfortable, you can also add some low-fiber foods throughout the day to increase your nutritional intake and avoid the boredom of just drinking. Then, eat a variety of foods after your competition to round out your nutrition for the day.

OF SPECIAL CONCERN TO POWERLIFTERS AND WEIGHTLIFTERS

As a powerlifter or weightlifter, you probably don't care much about getting ripped. Rather, you want to be as strong and as powerful as possible in your weight class. Here is what you should do to go strong for training and competition.

Load Your Muscles With Energy Sources

Carbohydrates and creatine are your best bets. Stay on a high-carb diet, supplemented with creatine. Take your creatine with carbs, as recommended in chapter 7, to supercharge your muscles with energy. Of the numerous studies now being published on creatine, this supplement is proving to be a sure thing for boosting strength and power.

You don't need to carbohydrate load. There is no scientific evidence showing that this method has any performance-enhancing benefit for strength athletes. Simply maintain a high-carb diet throughout your training and competition preparation. Going into competition well fueled is critical.

© Raymond J. Malace

A high-carb diet supplemented with creatine will help powerlifters and weightlifters prepare for competition.

Up Your Aerobics if You Need to Make Weight

While maintaining your high-carb diet, increase your aerobic exercise. This will help you lose fat to qualify for your weight class. You may need to decrease your calories slightly, too. If so, give yourself plenty of time to make weight—at least 10 to 12 weeks. If your contest is fast approaching, you can cut your calories down to 20 per kilogram of body weight a day. That will result in a three- to four-pound weight loss a week. But keep in mind that you may lose some muscle mass, too.

If you do cut to 20 calories per kilogram of body weight a day, stay on this regimen for no longer than seven days. Prolonged restrictive dieting slows your resting metabolic rate and your ability to burn fat.

Avoid Dangerous Make-Weight Practices

Prior to a meet, it is fairly common for some lifters to exercise in rubberized suits or sit in steam and sauna baths for extended periods—all without drinking much water. This practice can lead to dehydration so severe that it can harm the kidneys and heart. Dehydrated lifters usually do poorly in competition.

Nor is fasting a good idea, even for a day or two. You'll lose water rapidly—and gain the health problems caused by dehydration. Glycogen depletion sets in, too, making it virtually impossible to perform well on competition day.

ON WITH THE SHOW!

If you follow these guidelines as best you can, you will be amazed by how easy contest preparation can be. Within just a few months, you will achieve contest-ready condition. So get started—off with the body fat, and on with the show!

Sport Nutrition Fact vs. Fiction: Insulin: A Magic Bullet?

One of the most powerful and multifunction hormones in the human body is insulin. It increases the uptake and use of glucose by cells, including muscle cells. It has an anabolic (tissue-building) effect on the body by promoting protein formation. It joins forces with human growth hormone to promote growth. And, on the downside, it promotes fat synthesis.

Medically, the drug insulin is used to treat diabetes, a complex disease in which the pancreas does not produce enough insulin (a condition known as Type I diabetes), or the body doesn't use it properly (Type II diabetes). Type I diabetics require injections of insulin. Diabetes, in general, is the seventh leading cause of death in the United States, and about 11 million people have it.

In bodybuilding circles, insulin got a lot of attention in the '80s when an insulin-dependent diabetic bodybuilder won several major contests and came to prominence. Nondiabetic, healthy bodybuilders started experimenting with insulin to see if it would spark muscle growth. Thus, insulin joined the ranks of chemical muscle-building aids.

Bodybuilders and other strength athletes assumed that if insulin increased the body's use of glucose, then it could maximize glycogen storage. Wrong—there is no scientific evidence backing this. It is well known that you can stockpile plenty of glycogen with a high-carbohydrate diet. Nor is there any evidence that insulin promotes muscle growth.

Fooling around with insulin is downright dangerous. Injections of insulin, or any other synthetic hormone for that matter, can throw your natural hormonal balance out of whack and lead to a whole host of medical problems. Plus, there's the danger of insulin shock, which occurs when too much insulin is injected. You could become unconscious or have a seizure. Another complication is hypoglycemia, in which blood sugar drops dangerously low. Symptoms include tremors and sweating, and in extreme cases, convulsions, and loss of consciousness.

Unless you are being treated for Type I diabetes, leave insulin alone. Combined with hard-work training in the gym, the new nutritional discoveries now available to strength trainers and other athletes are all you need to build a winning physique.

Chapter 10

DESIGNING YOUR PERSONAL POWER-EATING PLAN

When strength-training athletes follow a healthy diet, they demonstrate what an amazing machine the human body is. Until recently, most sport scientists and physicians felt that strength training played little role in health maintenance. But now we know that, when combined with a healthful diet, strength training is essential not only for lifelong health, but to maintain physical independence as we age.

Unfortunately, too many strength-training athletes use unhealthy dietary practices, and possibly even drugs, with the hope of cheating time and rapidly achieving their goals. They may cheat time in the short run, but in the long run they are cheating themselves out of living a long, healthy life. There is no question that by following a sophisticated, scientifically based, healthy diet plan, you can build tremendous strength and muscle. Other successful athletes have done it. It will take longer than if you followed illegal and unhealthy strategies, but you'll live to enjoy it.

THE PLAN

Even though you are an active person, you are still human, and your basic nutrient requirements are generally the same as those of the rest of the human race, except, of course, for energy. To supply your body with the nutrients that you need every day, eat in virtually the same style as recommended in the USDA Food Guide Pyramid, but pump up the volume. In other words, to get in all the calories you need, you will probably need to eat more servings than recommended in the guide. As long as you eat a variety of foods from all the food groups, and you consume enough energy to meet your daily needs, you will most likely eat the amount of nutrients that your body requires. That's the whole concept behind the pyramid.

Proportionally, depending on the total calories in your diet, the nutrients should fall out at around 10 to 12 percent protein, 70 to 73 percent carb, and 16 to 20 percent fat during your training and maintenance phases. Tapering phases for bodybuilders or athletes trying to make weight will be different.

Learn to read labels. The nutrition facts labels on foods will tell you exactly how much protein, carb, and fat, and sometimes the types of fat that are found in the food you're eating. You might also want to purchase a book or software that can give you the nutrient breakdown of foods.

```
┌─────────────────────────────────────────┐
│ Nutrition Facts                          │
│ Serving Size ½ cup (114g)                │
│ Servings Per Container 4                  │
├─────────────────────────────────────────┤
│ Amount Per Serving                        │
│ Calories 260    Calories from Fat 120     │
├─────────────────────────────────────────┤
│                        % Daily Value*     │
│ Total Fat 13g                      20%    │
│   Saturated Fat 5g                 25%    │
│ Cholesterol 30mg                   10%    │
│ Sodium 660mg                       28%    │
│ Total Carbohydrate 31g             11%    │
│   Dietary Fiber 0g                  0%    │
│   Sugars 5g                               │
│ Protein 5g                                │
├─────────────────────────────────────────┤
│ Vitamin A 4%             Vitamin C 2%     │
│ Calcium 15%                  Iron 4%      │
├─────────────────────────────────────────┤
│ *Percent Daily Values are based on a 2000 │
│ calorie diet. Your daily values may be    │
│ higher or lower depending on your calorie │
│ needs.                                    │
│              Calories:   2000    2500     │
│ Total Fat    Less than   65g     80g      │
│   Sat. Fat   Less than   20g     25g      │
│ Cholesterol  Less than   300mg   300mg    │
│ Sodium       Less than   2400mg  2400mg   │
│ Total Carbohydrate       300g    375g     │
│   Dietary Fiber          25g     30g      │
│ Calories per gram:                        │
│ Fat 9 • Carbohydrate 4 • Protein 4        │
└─────────────────────────────────────────┘
```

Food nutrition label.

If you are trying to achieve the greatest strength and muscle-gain goals, use the following guidelines when designing your diet.

1. Figure Out Your Calorie Needs Based on Present Body Weight

As your weight changes, energy and nutrients must be recalculated.

Training to maintain muscle: 44 calories per kilogram of body weight a day for men (3,608 calories a day for a 180 pound man). Women may be able to increase muscle at 44 calories per kilogram of body weight a day (2,398 calories for a 120 pound woman), and maintain at about 38 to 40 calories per kilogram of body weight a day

(2,071 to 2,180 calories). The larger and more muscular a woman, the more calories she can handle for maintenance. Some of this is trial and error with women, since all of the research has been done on men. For the rest of the phases, women should generally choose the lower end of the calorie ranges. This diet is great for bodybuilders, power-lifters and weightlifters, as well as for recreational strength trainers.

Building: 52 to 60 calories per kilogram of body weight a day, depending on intensity of training (4,264 to 4,920 calories for a 180 pound man; 2,834 to 3,270 calories for a 120 pound woman). Start low and add as needed. This diet is good for all competitive and recreational strength trainers.

Tapering for competition (10–12 weeks of precontest dieting): 33 to 38 calories per kilogram of body weight a day (2,706 to 3,116 calories for a 180 pound man; 1,798 to 2,071 calories for a 120 pound woman). Because it is more difficult for women to lose fat than men, women should choose the lower calorie range (decrease about 500 calories a day from maintenance calorie levels, and increase aerobic exercise to burn about 500 calories a day). This recommendation is primarily for bodybuilders.

Cutting (seven days maximum): 30 calories per kilogram of body weight a day for women (1,635 calories for a 120 pound woman) and 33 calories per kilogram of body weight a day for men (2,706 calories for a 180 pound man). Use this approach only when absolutely necessary. This diet is only for bodybuilders or others trying to make a weight class, not for powerlifters or weightlifters.

For powerlifters and weightlifters trying to make a weight class: After dieting to build muscle, go back to the maintenance diet for two weeks prior to your meet, and use your goal weight for the calculations. This will allow for loss of body fat, without loss of muscle, strength, or power. This strategy is also a good basic diet for the overweight strength trainer who wants to lose body fat.

2. Figure Your Protein Needs

Bodybuilders:

Maintenance: 1.2 to 1.3 grams per kilogram of body weight a day

Building: 1.4 to 1.8 grams per kilogram of body weight a day

Tapering: 1.8 grams per kilogram of body weight a day

Cutting: 1.8 to 2.0 grams per kilogram of body weight a day (2.0 grams for those eating mostly vegetarian)

Strength and speed athletes:

Maintenance: 1.2 to 1.3 grams per kilogram of body weight a day

Building: 1.4 to 1.8 grams per kilogram of body weight a day

Athletes who strength train in addition to their regular sport (cross-trainers): 1.4 to 1.7 grams per kilogram of body weight a day

3. Figure Your Carbohydrate Needs

Calculate your carbs as 8 to 10 grams per kilogram of body weight a day, with strength trainers needing closer to 8 grams for maintenance and 9 grams per kilogram of body weight a day for building, intense cross-trainers needing closer to 10, and bodybuilders needing 8 grams for maintenance and 9 grams for building.

During tapering and cutting phases, calculate carbohydrate needs at 65 percent of total daily calories.

4. Figure Your Fat Needs

Basically, the rest of your calories will be 16 to 20 percent of your total calories. Fat sources should be predominantly mono- and polyunsaturated, and much less saturated fat. Review chapter 4 for how to figure out grams of fat.

5. Fluid Intake

Drink a quart of fluid for every 1,000 calories of food you eat. Consume more in hot, humid weather or at high altitude. Avoid caffeine and alcohol, which are dehydrating. Follow these additional guidelines.

- Fluids should be cool.
- For exercise lasting an hour or less, water is sufficient for replacing lost fluids.
- If flavoring increases palatability, then flavored drinks should be used.
- For exercise lasting more than an hour, carbohydrate-electrolyte sport drinks containing 4 to 8 percent carbohydrates (grams per 100 milliliters) are best. Carbohydrates can be glucose, sucrose, or maltodextrins. Fructose should

not be the sole or primary carbohydrate, but is acceptable in smaller amounts.

- Drink two cups of water two hours before exercise.
- Drink four to six ounces every 15 to 20 minutes during exercise.
- Drink at least two cups of fluid for every pound of body weight lost during exercise.

6. Supplements

Liquid: Carbohydrate-electrolyte beverages (previously discussed).

Meal replacers: These are good to use as balanced snacks and, after strength-training exercise, to consume carbohydrate-protein combinations for potential muscle-building enhancement. They are also great to use on the day of contests to avoid looking or feeling too full. Don't forget to figure the calories, protein, fat, and carbohydrate from these supplements into your dietary allowances.

Vitamins and minerals: Daily antioxidant multivitamin/mineral tablet may be unnecessary during maintenance and building phases, but might be helpful during tapering, especially for women.

Vitamin E: 100 to 400 IU supplement is recommended.

Calcium: Men and women who avoid dairy products due to taste or physical discomfort should take 800 to 1,200 milligrams a day. It is best to try to get as much calcium as possible from food.

Creatine: This supplement is definitely worth a try, especially for full or partial vegetarians since creatine is found naturally in meat. Follow the dosing plan in chapter 7.

7. Time Your Meals Appropriately for Best Results

- Eat small, frequent meals to promote calorie burning versus fat storage. Five to six meals a day are best—more if your calories are higher than 3,000 a day. Make sure to eat breakfast if you work out in the morning. Eat smaller meals in the evening. It is best to eat two to three hours before exercise. This meal should be high in carbs and low in fat (except when you are tapering).

- Replace your glycogen stores by consuming high-glycemic index foods within 15 minutes to two hours following exercise.
- Promote muscle building by consuming a carbohydrate-protein formula within two hours following strength-training exercise.

For Competitive Bodybuilders:

Here's an at-a-glance review of guidelines to follow if you're preparing for a contest.

Tapering phase: Begin this phase 10 to 12 weeks prior to your contest. Decrease calories and increase aerobic exercise. The more aerobically fit you are, the more fat you'll be able to burn. Aerobics should be part of your all-around program, but aerobic exercise is even more important now. During the tapering phase, reduce calories by reducing carbohydrates and fats. Avoid carbohydrates within four hours before aerobic exercise to maximize your fat-burning potential.

Cutting phase (one week prior to your contest): If you're not looking as ripped as you would like, follow the cutting program of 30 to 33 calories per kilogram of body weight a day for one week. This will allow for a final loss of three to four pounds, as long as you keep your aerobic training intense. Make sure to up your protein intake to 1.8 to 2.0 grams per kilogram of body weight a day. Drop calories by reducing carbs to 65 percent of total calories and by further reducing your fat intake.

Use the cutting phase to get ripped.

© Raymond J. Malace

STICKING TO YOUR PLAN

For these power-eating strategies to work, you have to stick to your plan. Design your diet with the foods that you like. Use the sample diets in chapter 11 to help you design your personal plan. If you don't like the foods you're supposed to eat, you won't stick to the plan. If you are using liquid supplements, try different brands and flavors, and find the ones that you like.

Pay attention to your body. Plan to eat when you are hungry. You might want to pick specific times of the day to eat, rather than depending on the pace of each different day. But also be aware of whether you are hungry or thirsty. Sometimes we confuse thirst with hunger. Keep food and drink on hand wherever you go. The most successful strength trainers always have a backpack full of food and drink. It goes with them everywhere. This way, they can stick to their timed eating patterns, and if they get hungry, they are not dependent on vending machines or other snack foods that will be high in fat and sodium.

During your tapering phase, you might find it difficult to eat at restaurants, and especially difficult to travel. If you must do either, try to find restaurants that specialize in healthy fare. They should be able to easily adjust their menu to meet your personal needs. Don't forget to ask what is in the recipe. A menu description may be misleading. You can even ask for foods that are not on the menu. They may be able to accommodate your request.

Remember to always recalculate your requirements based on your present weight. If you have gained weight during a building or bulking phase, and now want to taper, use your new weight, rather than that of the prebulking phase.

No one can do this for you. You know that to get big and strong, you have to work your body hard. You also have to fuel your body to grow. And this is the best way. Plan your diet and stick to it. You will be thrilled with how you feel, how you look, and how you perform.

Sport Nutrition Fact vs. Fiction: The Nutrition in Fast Foods

If yours is an on-the-go lifestyle, you probably have to order fast food every now and then. The key is to make the right choices—those that are low in fat and high in nutrition. Fortunately, fast-food restaurants today cater to the low-fat preferences of consumers.

To help you make healthy choices, table 10.1 lists some "best bets" at fast-food restaurants.

Here are some additional fast-food tips to keep you on track:

- Always order the regular-sized sandwiches because they are lower in fat.
- In place of a bigger sandwich, order a salad, low-fat milk, and low-fat frozen yogurt to complete your meal.
- Stay away from fried foods.
- Don't eat the high-fat tortilla shells from taco salads.
- Request that sour cream and secret sauces be left off your order.
- Top your baked potato with chili instead of fatty cheese sauce.
- Whatever you order, order just one!

TABLE 10.1 Healthy Fast Food

Food	Calories	Percent of fat
Arby's		
Blueberry muffin	200	25
Plain baked potato	240	7
Chicken fajita pita	272	31
Grilled chicken barbecue	378	34
Lite chicken deluxe	263	21
Lite ham deluxe	255	19
Lite roast beef deluxe	294	31
Lite roast turkey deluxe	260	17
French dip roast beef	345	32
Beef with vegetables and barley soup	96	26
Old-fashioned chicken noodle soup	99	16
Tomato Florentine soup	84	16
Burger King		
Angel hair pasta with cheese (Weight Watchers)	210	21
Angel hair pasta without cheese (Weight Watchers)	160	11
BK broiler sandwich	267	27
Broiled chicken sandwich (no dressing)	140	26

(continued)

TABLE 10.1 *(continued)*

Food	Calories	Percent of fat
Burger King *(cont.)*		
Chunky chicken salad (no dressing)	142	25
Veggie sticks	60	15
Chocolate brownie (Weight Watchers)	100	27
Mocha pie (Weight Watchers)	160	28
McDonald's		
Low-fat shakes	320	5
Cheerios	80	11
Wheaties	90	10
English muffin with spread	170	21
Chunky chicken salad (no dressing)	150	24
Lite vinaigrette dressing (1 tbsp)	12	38
Hamburger	255	32
Pizza Hut		
Cheese pizza (2 medium slices)	518	35
Cheese pan pizza (2 medium slices)	492	33
Taco Bell		
Bean burrito	387	33
Chicken burrito	334	32
Combination burrito	407	35
Wendy's		
Apple Danish	360	35
Chili (small)	190	28
Chili (large)	290	28
Plain baked potato	300	2
Caesar side salad	160	34
Grilled chicken sandwich	290	22
Junior hamburger	270	30

Chapter 11

SAMPLE STRENGTH-TRAINING DIETS

To help you map out your own strength-training diet, here are several sample diets. All of the diets are based on the needs of a 120 pound (54.5 kilogram) woman and a 180 pound (81.8 kilogram) man. To make the diet user friendly, some numbers are rounded off to the nearest 10 or 100. To change pounds to kilograms, divide pounds by 2.2.

MAINTENANCE DIET

120 lb. Woman: 2,400 Calories

	Grams	Calories	% of Calories
PROTEIN (1.2g/kg/d)	65	260	11
CARBOHYDRATES (8g/kg/d)	436	1,744	73
FAT (g)	44	396	16

180 lb. Man: 3,600 Calories

	Grams	Calories	% of Calories
PROTEIN (1.2g/kg/d)	98	392	11
CARBOHYDRATES (8g/kg/d)	654	2,616	73
FAT (g)	66	594	16

(For bodybuilders, recreational strength trainers, powerlifters, weight-lifters; also, for those using a goal weight, a precompetition fat-loss diet for powerlifters and weightlifters [44 calories/kg/d].)

BUILDING DIET

120 lb. Woman: 2,800 Calories

	Grams	Calories	% of Calories
PROTEIN (1.4g/kg/d)	76	304	11
CARBOHYDRATES (9g/kg/d)	491	1,964	70
FAT (g)	59	531	19

180 lb. Man: 4,250 Calories

	Grams	Calories	% of Calories
PROTEIN (1.4g/kg/d)	115	460	11
CARBOHYDRATES (9g/kg/d)	736	2,944	69
FAT (g)	94	846	20

(For bodybuilders, powerlifters, weightlifters, and other serious strength trainers [52 calories/kg/d].)

TAPERING DIET

120 lb. Woman: 1,900 Calories

	Grams	Calories	% of Calories
PROTEIN (1.8g/kg/d)	98	392	21
CARBOHYDRATES (65% of calories)	309	1,236	65
FAT (g)	30	270	14

180 lb. Man: 3,100 Calories

	Grams	Calories	% of Calories
PROTEIN (1.8g/kg/d)	147	588	19
CARBOHYDRATES (65% of calories)	503	2,012	65
FAT (g)	56	504	16

(For bodybuilders: Because it is more difficult for women to lose fat than men, calorie levels are different here for men [38 calories/kg/d] and women [35 calories/kg/d].)

CUTTING DIET

120 lb. Woman: 1,635 Calories

	Grams	Calories	% of Calories
PROTEIN (1.8g/kg/d)	98	392	24
CARBOHYDRATES (65% of calories)	266	1,064	65
FAT (g)	20	180	11

180 lb. Man: 2,700 Calories

	Grams	Calories	% of Calories
PROTEIN (1.8g/kg/d)	147	588	22
CARBOHYDRATES (65% of calories)	439	1,756	65
FAT (g)	40	360	13

(Since it is more difficult for women to lose fat than men, calorie levels are different here for men [33 calories/kg/d] and women [30 calories/kg/d]. Stay on this diet no longer than seven days.)

SERVING SIZE GUIDELINES FOR KEY FOOD GROUPS

These are a representation of the foods and serving sizes for each food group. For a more extensive list, contact the American Dietetic Association (1-800-366-1655) to purchase *Exchange Lists for Meal Planning*, Revised Edition, 1995.

FOOD GROUP	SERVING SIZE
Starch	1 slice bread; 1/2 cup cooked cereal, pasta, or starchy vegetable; 1/3 cup rice; 1 ounce ready-to-eat cereal; 1/2 bun, bagel, or English muffin; 1 small roll; 3-4 small or 2 large crackers
Fruit	1 small to medium fresh fruit; 1/2 cup of canned or fresh fruit or fruit juice; 1/4 cup of dried fruit; 1/2 grapefruit; 1 melon wedge
Nonfat milk	1 cup of nonfat milk
Other carbohydrates	These foods count as starches, fruits, or milks, and add variety to your diet. They may also contain one or more fat choices.
Vegetables	1/2 cup cooked vegetables or vegetable juice; 1 cup raw vegetables
Meat & meat substitutes	1 ounce meat, fish, poultry, or cheese; 1/2 cup beans, peas, and lentils (count as 1 starch plus 1 very lean meat)
Very lean	White meat skinless poultry; cod, flounder, haddock, halibut, trout; tuna fresh or canned in water; all shellfish; cheese with 1 gram or less fat per ounce; processed sandwich meats with 1 gram or less fat per ounce; egg whites

Lean	USDA Select or Choice grades of lean beef, pork, lamb, or veal, trimmed of fat; dark meat skinless poultry or white meat chicken with skin; oysters, salmon, catfish, sardines, tuna canned in oil; 4.5% cottage cheese (1/4 cup), grated Parmesan (2 tablespoons), cheese with 3 grams or less fat per ounce; processed sandwich meat with 3 grams or less fat per ounce
Medium fat	Most styles of beef, pork, lamb, veal, trimmed of fat, prime grades trimmed of fat; dark meat chicken with skin, ground turkey or ground chicken; any fish product; cheese with 5 grams or less fat per ounce; whole egg; soy milk (1 cup); tempeh (1/4 cup); tofu (4 ounces or 1/2 cup)
Fat	1 teaspoon butter, margarine, vegetable oil; 1 tablespoon regular salad dressing; 2 tablespoons reduced-fat salad dressing; 1 tablespoon reduced-fat mayonnaise; 2 tablespoons reduced-fat cream cheese; 1/8 medium avocado; 8 olives; 6-10 nuts; 2 teaspoons peanut butter or tahini; 1 tablespoon seeds
Liquid supplements	Nutrient values are based on Gatorade carbohydrate-electrolyte, high-carbohydrate, and meal-replacer products (Gatorade, GatorLode, GatorPro) and Kleiner's Muscle-Building Formula

* If you work out more than once a day, split up carb-electrolyte beverage servings for each workout. Do not add more. Use water to replace extra fluids.

Kleiner's Muscle-Building Formula

8 ounces nonfat milk

1 packet Carnation Instant Breakfast

1 banana

1 tablespoon peanut butter

Blend until smooth. One serving contains 438 calories, 70 grams carbohydrate, 17 grams protein, 10 grams fat

2,400 CALORIE MAINTENANCE DIET

FOOD GROUP	NUMBER OF SERVINGS
Starch	7
Fruit	4
Other carbohydrates	1 cookie or 1 small 2-inch square brownie or 1/2 cup light ice cream or 1 unfrosted piece of cake or 1 granola bar or 5 vanilla wafers or 1/3 cup low-fat frozen yogurt; and 1 cup low-fat yogurt with fruit
Vegetables	3
Meat & substitutes	
Lean	2
Medium fat	1

Fat   1

Liquid supplements

   Carb-electrolyte replacer   4 servings (32 ounces)

   High-carb replacer   1 serving (11.6 ounces)

   Kleiner's Muscle-Building   1 serving
   Formula

Breakfast	1 bagel
	1 cup low-fat yogurt
	1 cup orange juice
Snack	high-carb replacer
	3, 2 1/2-inch square graham crackers
Lunch	1 hard boiled egg
	1 cup salad greens
	1/2 tomato
	2 tablespoons fat-free Italian dressing
	2 rice cakes
	1 apple
	water
Snack	1 1/2 ounces pretzels
	1 small banana
	water
Workout	carb-electrolyte replacer (32 ounces)
After workout	Kleiner's Muscle-Building Formula
Dinner	1/2 cup pasta sauce with 2 ounces ground round
	1 cup cooked pasta
	1 cup broccoli
	1/2 cup light ice cream
	water

3,600 CALORIE MAINTENANCE DIET

FOOD GROUP	NUMBER OF SERVINGS
Starch	8
Fruit	5
Nonfat milk	1
Other carbohydrates	1 cup low-fat yogurt with fruit; and 3 tablespoons jam or jelly or syrup; and 2/3 cup fat-free frozen yogurt; and 2 granola bars
Vegetables	5
Meat & substitutes	
Lean	3
Medium fat	2
Fat	4
Liquid supplements	
Carb-electrolyte replacer	5 servings (40 ounces)
High-carb replacer	2 servings (23.2 ounces)
Meal replacer	1 serving

Breakfast	1 cup shredded wheat
	1/4 cup raisins
	1 cup nonfat milk
	1/2 cup orange juice
Snack	1 bagel
	2 tablespoons low-fat cream cheese
	3 tablespoons jam or jelly
	1 serving high-carbohydrate beverage

Lunch	2 hard boiled eggs
	3 cups tossed salad
	2 tablespoons low-fat salad dressing
	2 breadsticks (4-inch long)
	1 apple
Snack	2 granola bars
	1 cup low-fat yogurt
	1 serving high-carb replacer beverage
Workout	carbohydrate-electrolyte replacer (40 ounces)
After workout	meal replacer
Dinner	3 ounces dark meat chicken (no skin)
	1/2 cup sweet potato or yam with 1 teaspoon butter
	1 cup asparagus
	2/3 cup brown rice
	1 cup stir-fried pea pods in 1 teaspoon oil
	2/3 cup fat-free frozen yogurt with 1/2 sliced banana and 1/2 cup sliced straw-berries
	water

2,800 CALORIE BUILDING DIET

FOOD GROUP	NUMBER OF SERVINGS
Starch	7
Fruit	5
Other carbohydrates	1 cookie or 1 small 2-inch square brownie or 1/2 cup light ice cream or 1 unfrosted piece of cake or 1 granola bar or 5 vanilla wafers or

Other carbohydrates (cont.)	1/3 cup low-fat frozen yogurt; and 1 cup low-fat yogurt with fruit; and 2 tablespoons jam/jelly/syrup
Vegetables	3
Meat & substitutes	
Lean	4
Medium fat	1
Fat	1 plus 20 peanuts or 4 teaspoons peanut butter
Liquid supplements	
Carb-electrolyte replacer	5 servings (40 ounces)
High-carb replacer	1 serving (11.6 ounces)
Kleiner's Muscle-Building Formula	1 serving

Breakfast	1 egg
	2 slices raisin toast
	1 cup orange juice
Snack	1 cup low-fat yogurt
	1 serving high-carb replacer
Lunch	1 bagel
	4 teaspoons peanut butter
	2 tablespoons jelly or jam
	5 baby carrots
	3 ounces grapes (17 small)
	1 cup melon cubes
	water
Snack	3 cups low-fat microwave or no fat added popcorn
	1/2 cup pineapple juice
Workout	carb-electrolyte replacer (40 ounces)
After workout	Kleiner's Muscle-Building Formula

Dinner	4 ounces grilled salmon with 1 teaspoon butter
	2/3 cup wild rice
	1 sliced tomato
	1 cup kale
	1 small 2-inch square brownie
	water

4,250 CALORIE BUILDING DIET

FOOD GROUP	NUMBER OF SERVINGS
Starch	8
Fruit	6
Nonfat milk	1
Other carbohydrates	1 cup low-fat yogurt with fruit; and 3 tablespoons jam or jelly or syrup; and 2/3 cup fat-free frozen yogurt; and 2 granola bars
Vegetables	5
Meat & substitutes	
Lean	3
Medium fat	2
Fat	7
Liquid supplements	
Carb-electrolyte replacer	5 servings (40 ounces)
High-carb replacer	2 servings (23.2 ounces)
Meal replacer	1 serving
Kleiner's Muscle-Building Formula	1 serving

Breakfast	Kleiner's Muscle-Building Formula
	6 4-inch round pancakes
	3 tablespoons syrup
	1 cup orange juice
Snack	1 serving high-carb replacer
	1 cup low-fat yogurt
Lunch	1 6-inch round pita bread stuffed with 3 ounces low-fat cheese (<3 grams fat/ounce), sprouts, sliced tomato, sliced red pepper, 1/8 avocado, 1 tablespoon nonfat ranch dressing
	carrot sticks
	1 large pear
	1 cup nonfat milk
Snack	1 serving high-carb replacer
	2 granola bars
	8 dried apricot halves
Workout	40 ounces carb-electrolyte replacer
After workout	meal replacer
Dinner	3 cups stir-fried vegetables with 1/2 pound tofu
	1 tablespoon oil
	1 cup brown rice
	2/3 cup fat-free frozen yogurt with 1 cup raspberries

1,900 CALORIE TAPERING DIET

FOOD GROUP	NUMBER OF SERVINGS
Starch	7
Fruit	4
Nonfat milk	1

Vegetables	3
Meat & substitutes	
Very lean	5
Lean	2
Fat	1
Liquid supplements	
Carb-electrolyte replacer	3 servings (24 ounces)
Kleiner's Muscle-Building Formula	1 serving

Breakfast	1 cup oatmeal
	2 tablespoons raisins
	1 cup nonfat milk
	1/2 cup orange juice
Snack	12 ounces carb-electrolyte replacer
Snack	12 ounces carb-electrolyte replacer
	16 animal crackers or 6, 2 1/2-inch square graham crackers
Lunch	1/2 cup cottage cheese
	1/2 cup applesauce
	1 sliced tomato
	1 slice whole wheat bread
	water
Snack	celery with 2 teaspoons peanut butter
Workout	water
After workout	Kleiner's Muscle-Building Formula
Dinner	5 ounces white-fleshed fish or shellfish
	1 cup asparagus
	2/3 cup brown rice
	1 slice or 1 1/4 cup cubed watermelon

3,100 CALORIE TAPERING DIET

FOOD GROUP	NUMBER OF SERVINGS
Starch	8
Fruit	5
Nonfat milk	1
Other carbohydrates	1 cup low-fat yogurt with fruit; and 2 tablespoons jam or jelly or syrup; and 2/3 cup fat-free frozen yogurt; and 2 granola bars
Vegetables	6
Meat & substitutes	
Very lean	5
Lean	6
Fat	2
Liquid supplements	
High-carb replacer	1 serving (11.6 ounces)
Meal replacer	1 serving

Breakfast	1 cup shredded wheat
	1/4 cup raisins
	1 cup nonfat milk
	1/2 cup orange juice
Snack	2 granola bars
Snack	1 bagel with 2 tablespoons jam or jelly
	1 cup low-fat yogurt
	1 serving high-carb replacer

Lunch	5 ounces white fleshed fish or shellfish or tuna in water
	3 cups tossed salad
	2 tablespoons fat-free Italian dressing
	1 large whole wheat roll
	3/4 cup fresh pineapple or 1/2 cup canned pineapple
Snack	celery sticks with 4 teaspoons peanut butter
	water
Workout	water
After workout	meal replacer
Dinner	6 ounces lean meat trimmed of fat (round, sirloin, flank steak, tenderloin; rib roast; T-bone, porterhouse)
	1 cup acorn squash
	1 medium corn-on-the-cob
	2 cups asparagus
	2/3 cup fat-free frozen yogurt with 1/2 cup sweet canned cherries
	water

1,635 CALORIE CUTTING DIET

FOOD GROUP	NUMBER OF SERVINGS
Starch	6
Fruit	2
Nonfat milk	1
Vegetables	3
Meat & substitutes	
Very lean	7
Liquid supplements	

Carb-electrolyte replacer	3 1/2 servings (28 ounces)
Kleiner's Muscle-Building Formula	1 serving

Breakfast	3/4 cup Kashi cereal
	2 tablespoons raisins
	1 cup nonfat milk
Snack	14 ounces carb-electrolyte replacer
Snack	14 ounces carb-electrolyte replacer
	8 animal crackers or 3, 2 1/2-inch square graham crackers
Lunch	1 6-inch round pita bread stuffed with 3 ounces tuna in water and 1 cup veggies
	1 small plum
	water
Workout	water
After workout	Kleiner's Muscle-Building Formula
Dinner	4 ounces chicken breast (no skin)
	1/3 cup brown rice
	1 cup asparagus
	1 cup tossed salad with balsamic vinegar and freshly ground black pepper for dressing
	3/4 cup whole strawberries

2,700 CALORIE CUTTING DIET

FOOD GROUP	NUMBER OF SERVINGS
Starch	8
Fruit	5
Nonfat milk	1
Other carbohydrates	1 cup low-fat yogurt with fruit; and 2 tablespoons jam or jelly or syrup
Vegetables	6

Meat & substitutes

Very lean	11

Fat   3

Liquid supplements

High-carb replacer	1 serving (11.6 ounces)
Meal replacer	1 serving

Breakfast	1 cup shredded wheat
	1/4 cup raisins
	1 cup nonfat milk
	1/2 cup orange juice
Snack	1 serving high-carb replacer
	1 bagel
	2 tablespoons jelly or jam
Lunch	5 ounces sliced turkey breast
	2 slices whole wheat bread
	3 lettuce leaves
	1 sliced tomato
	1 tablespoon low-fat mayonnaise
	1/2 cup raw mushrooms
	carrot sticks
	1 apple
	water
Snack	20 unsalted peanuts
	water
Workout	water
After workout	meal replacer
Dinner	6 ounces white-fleshed fish
	2/3 cup brown rice
	1 cup asparagus
	2 cups tossed salad with balsamic vinegar and freshly ground black pepper for dressing
	1 1/4 cups whole strawberries
	water

Indian Breakfast Salad

This delicious salad is served as a side dish in India, but makes a fast and fabulous breakfast. It is spiced with cardamom, but because of cardamom's price, unless you use it in other recipes, you may prefer to use cinnamon.

1/2 teaspoon butter

2 tablespoons slivered almonds

2 medium bananas, thinly sliced

4 tablespoons low-fat plain yogurt

3 tablespoons light sour cream

1 tablespoon honey

1/8 teaspoon ground cardamom
(or 1/4 teaspoon ground cinnamon)

1. Melt the butter in a small nonstick skillet over medium heat. Toast almonds, stirring frequently, until golden, about three minutes.

2. Meanwhile, in a medium bowl, mix bananas with yogurt, sour cream, honey, and cardamom. Add almonds and enjoy.

Makes two servings. Each serving contains 213 calories, 6 grams of protein (11%), 32 grams of carbohydrate (57%), 8 grams of fat (32%).

Breakfast Parfait

Make this artistic, high-powered breakfast portable by using plastic drinking cups with lids.

2 cups low-fat strawberry yogurt

1 cup low-fat granola

1 cup fresh berries (whatever is in season)

1. In two 16-ounce glass or plastic cups, layer the ingredients by adding 1/2 cup of the yogurt, 1/4 cup of the granola, and 1/4 cup of berries.

2. Repeat step 1, reserving a dollop of the yogurt for the top.

Makes two servings. Each serving contains 472 calories, 13 grams of protein (11%), 95 grams of carbohydrate (78%), 6 grams of fat (11%).

Peach Melba Yogurt Pops

These delicious pops can be prepared the night before to make a great light breakfast that you can easily hit the road with on a warm summer morning. If you don't want to bother with adding the sticks, just poke a fork into the pop when you are ready to eat.

1 cup sliced canned peaches in light syrup

1 cup low-fat raspberry yogurt

1 cup orange juice

1. Blend ingredients until smooth. Pour into four, 10-ounce plastic cups. Place in the freezer.

2. When mixture is partly frozen, insert sticks or plastic spoons.

Makes two servings. Each serving contains 249 calories, 6 grams of protein (10%), 53 grams of carbohydrate (86%), 1 gram of fat (4%).

Orange Cinnamon French Toast

This toast takes only slightly longer to prepare than the standard version that pops out of the toaster.

2 large eggs, lightly beaten

2 tablespoons orange juice

1/4 teaspoon ground cinnamon

vegetable cooking spray

4 slices whole wheat bread

1. In a shallow bowl, combine eggs, orange juice, and cinnamon.
2. Spray a nonstick skillet and heat over medium heat for one to two minutes, until hot. Dip bread into the mixture to coat both sides. Place bread slices in the skillet, pouring any extra egg mixture over them. Cook for about two minutes on each side or until browned.

Makes two servings. Each serving contains 254 calories, 13 grams of protein (20%), 35 grams of carbohydrate (53%), 8 grams of fat (27%).

Pineapple Cheese Danish

4 slices raisin bread

4 tablespoons canned unsweetened crushed pineapple, drained

1/2 cup (4 ounces) part-skim-milk ricotta cheese

1 teaspoon brown sugar

dash ground cinnamon

1. Spread each slice of bread with one ounce of cheese and top with pineapple. Combine brown sugar and cinnamon and sprinkle on top of the pineapple.

2. Broil in a toaster oven or under the broiler until sugar starts to bubble, about two minutes.

Makes two servings. Each serving contains 239 calories, 11 grams of protein (18%), 33 grams of carbohydrate (55%), 7 grams of fat (27%).

Strawberry Banana Smoothie

1 packet strawberry Carnation Instant Breakfast powder

1 cup low-fat strawberry banana yogurt

1 cup nonfat milk

2 ice cubes, crushed

1. Place all ingredients in a blender and process for one minute or until ice is blended. Drink immediately.

Makes two servings. Each serving contains 440 calories, 26 grams of protein (23%), 82 grams of carbohydrate (75%), 1 gram of fat (2%).

Fruit 'n' Cheese

1 small red apple, cored and sliced

1 small D'Anjou or Bartlett pear, cored and sliced

2 ounces thinly sliced cheddar cheese

4 slices whole wheat toast

1. Place apple and pear slices on bread and cover with cheese to make open-face sandwiches. Place under broiler or in toaster oven for two to three minutes or until cheese melts and bubbles.

Makes two servings. Each serving contains 396 calories, 14 grams of protein (14%), 56 grams of carbohydrate (57%), 13 grams of fat (29%).

REFERENCES

Akermark, C., I. Jacobs, M. Rasmusson, and J. Karlsson. 1996. Diet and muscle glycogen concentration in relation to physical performance in Swedish elite ice hockey players. *International Journal of Sport Nutrition* 6: 272–84.

Anderson, O. 1995. Burn, baby, burn. *Runner's World*, May, 38.

Andersson, B., et al. 1991. The effects of exercise training on body composition and metabolism in men and women. *International Journal of Obesity* 15: 75–81.

Applegate, L. 1992. Protein power. *Runner's World*, June, 22–24.

Balon, T.W., J.F. Horowitz, and K.M. Fitzsimmons. 1992. Effects of carbohydrate loading and weight lifting on muscle girth. *International Journal of Sports Nutrition* 2: 328–34.

Bean, A. 1996. Here's to your immunity. *Runner's World*, February, 23.

Bellisle, F., and C. Perez. 1994. Low-energy substitutes for sugars and fats in the human diet: impact on nutritional regulation. *Neuroscience Behavioral Review* 18: 197–205.

Bjorntorp, P. 1991. Importance of fat as a support nutrient for energy: metabolism of athletes. *Journal of Sports Sciences* 9: 71–76.

Brilla, L.R., and T.F. Haley. 1992. Effect of magnesium supplementation on strength training in humans. *Journal of the American College of Nutrition* 11: 326–29.

Brown, J. 1990. *The science of human nutrition*. San Diego: Harcourt Brace Jovanovich.

Brown, J., M.C. Crim, V.R. Young, and W.J. Evans. 1994. Increased energy requirements and changes in body composition with resistance training in older adults. *American Journal of Clinical Nutrition* 60: 167–75.

Bryner, R.W., R.C. Toffle, I.H. Ullrich, and R.A. Yeager. 1997. The effects of exercise intensity on body composition, weight loss, and dietary composition in women. *Journal of the American College of Nutrition* 16: 68–73.

Campbell, W.W., et al. 1995. Effects of resistance training and dietary protein intake on protein metabolism in older adults. *American Journal of Physiology* 268: E1143–53.

Chandler, R.M., H.K. Byrne, J.G. Patterson, and J.L. Ivy. 1994. Dietary supplements affect the anabolic hormones after weight training exercise. *Journal of Applied Physiology* 76: 839–45.

Charley, H. 1982. *Food Science*. New York: Wiley.

Clancy, S.P., et al. 1994. Effects of chromium picolinate supplementation on body composition, strength, and urinary chromium loss in football players. *International Journal of Sport Nutrition* 4: 142–53.

Clark, N. 1993. Athletes with amenorrhea. *The Physician and Sportsmedicine* 21: 45–48.

Clarkson, P.M. 1991. Nutritional ergogenic aids: chromium, exercise, and muscle mass. *International Journal of Sport Nutrition* 1: 289–93.

———. 1996. Nutrition for improved sports performance: current issues on ergogenic aids. *Sports Medicine* 21: 393–401.

Coleman, E. 1997. Carbohydrate unloading: a reality check. *The Physician and Sportsmedicine* 25: 97–98.

Collomp, K., A. Ahmaidi, M. Audran, and C. Prefaut. 1992. Benefits of caffeine ingestion on sprint performance in trained and untrained swimmers. *European Journal of Applied Physiology* 64: 377–80.

———. 1991. Effects of caffeine ingestion on performance and anaerobic metabolism during the Wingate Test. *International Journal of Sports Medicine* 12: 439–43.

Convertino, V.A., L.E. Armstrong, E.F. Coyle, G.W. Mack, M.N. Sawka, L.C. Senay, Jr., and W.M. Sherman. 1996. American College of Sports Medicine position stand: Exercise and fluid replacement. *Medicine and Science in Sports and Exercise* 28(1): i.

Coyle, E.F. 1997. Fuels for sport performance. In *Perspectives in exercise science and sports medicine*, eds. D. Lamb and R. Murray. Carmel, IN: Cooper Publishing Group.

————. 1995. Fat metabolism during exercise. *Sports Science Exchange* 8: 1–7.

Deschenes, M.R., and W.J. Kraemer. 1989. The biochemical basis of muscular fatigue. *National Strength and Conditioning Association Journal* 11: 41–44.

Dias, V. 1990. Effects of feeding and energy balance in adult humans. *Metabolism* 39: 887–91.

Dimeff, R.J. 1996. Drugs and sports: prescription and non-prescription. Paper presented at symposium, Sports Medicine for the Rheumatologist. Meeting of the American College of Rheumatology, 19 May, at Phoenix, Arizona.

————. 1993. Steroids and other performance enhancers. In *Clinical preventive medicine*, eds. R.N. Matzen and R.S. Lang. St Louis: Mosby.

Dorant, E., et al. 1996. Consumption of onions and a reduced risk of stomach carcinoma. *Gastroenterology* 110: 12–20.

Essen-Gustavsson, B., and P.A. Tesch. 1990. Glycogen and triglyceride utilization in relation to muscle metabolic characteristics in men performing heavy-resistance exercise. *European Journal of Applied Physiology* 61: 5–10.

Evans, W. 1996. The protective role of antioxidants in exercise-induced oxidative stress. Keynote address given at 13th Annual SCAN Symposium, 28 April, at Scottsdale, Arizona.

Fawcett, J.P., et al. 1996. The effect of oral vanadyl sulfate on body composition and performance in weight-training athletes. *International Journal of Sport Nutrition* 6: 382–90.

Fogelholm, M. 1992. Micronutrient status in females during a 24-week fitness-type exercise program. *Annals of Nutrition and Metabolism* 36: 209–18.

Foley, D. 1984. Best health bets from the B team. *Prevention*, April, 62–67.

Frentsos, J.A., and J.R. Baer. 1997. Increased energy and nutrient intake during training and competition improves elite triathletes' endurance performance. *International Journal of Sport Nutrition* 7: 61–71.

Frey-Hewitt, K.M., K.M. Vranizan, D.M. Dreon, and P.D. Wood. 1990. The effect of weight loss by dieting or exercise on resting metabolic rate in overweight men. *International Journal of Obesity* 14: 327–34.

Friedl, K.E., et al. 1994. Lower limit of body fat in healthy active men. *Journal of Applied Physiology* 77: 933–40.

Gillette, C.A., R.C. Bullough, and C.L. Melby. 1994. Postexercise energy expenditure in response to acute aerobic or resistive exercise. *International Journal of Sport Nutrition* 4: 347–60.

Gillman, M.W., et al. 1995. Protective effect of fruits and vegetables on development of stroke in men. *Journal of the American Medical Association* 273: 1113–17.

Giovannuci, E., et al. 1995. Intake of carotenoids and retinol in relation to risk of prostate cancer. *Journal of the National Cancer Institute* 87: 1767–76.

Gornall, J., and R.G. Villani. 1996. Short-term changes in body composition and metabolism with severe dieting and resistance exercise. *International Journal of Sport Nutrition* 6: 285–94.

Green, A.L., E. Hultman, I.A. MacDonald, D.A. Sewell, and P.L. Greenhaff. 1996. Carbohydrate ingestion augments skeletal muscle creatine accumulation during creatine supplementation in humans. *American Journal of Physiology* 271: E821–26.

Green, N.R. and A.A. Ferrando. 1994. Plasma boron and the effects of boron supplementation in males. *Environmental Health Perspective* Supplement 7: 73–77.

Harberson, D.A. 1988. Weight gain and body composition of weightlifters: effect of high-calorie supplementation vs. anabolic steroids. In *Report of the Ross Laboratories Symposium on Muscle development: nutritional alternatives to anabolic steroids*, eds. W.E. Garrett Jr. and T.E. Malone. Columbus, OH: Ross Laboratories.

Harvard Heart Letter. Editor. 1996. The new diet pills: fairly but not completely safe. 7: 1–2.

Hartung, G.H., et al. 1990. Effect of alcohol dose on plasma lipoprotein subfractions and lipolytic enzyme activity in active and inactive men. *Metabolism* 39: 81–86.

Health, M.K., ed. 1982. *Diet manual*, including a vegetarian meal plan. 6th ed. Loma Linda, CA 92345: Seventh Day Adventist Dietetic Association, P.O. Box 75.

Jacobsen, B.H. 1990. Effect of amino acids on growth hormone release. *The Physician and Sportsmedicine* 18: 68.

Jennings, E. 1995. Folic acid as a cancer-preventing agent. *Medical Hypotheses* 45: 297–303.

Kanter, M.M., L.A. Nolte, and J.O. Holloszy. 1993. Effects of an antioxidant vitamin mixture on lipid peroxidation at rest and postexercise. *Journal of Applied Physiology* 74: 965–69.

Keim, N.L., A.Z. Belko, and T.F. Barbieri. 1996. Body fat percentage and gender: associations with exercise energy expenditure, substrate utilization, and mechanical work efficiency. *International Journal of Sport Nutrition* 6: 356–69.

Keim, N.L., T.F. Barbieri, M.D. Van Loan, and B.L. Anderson. 1990. Energy expenditure and physical performance in overweight women: response to training with and without caloric restriction. *Metabolism* 39: 651–58.

Keith, R.E., K.A. O'Keefe, D.L. Blessing, and G.D. Wilson. 1991. Alterations in dietary carbohydrate, protein, and fat intake and mood state in trained female cyclists. *Medicine and Science in Sports and Exercise.* 23: 212–16.

Kendrick, Z.V., M.B. Affrime, and D.T. Lowenthal. 1993. Effect of ethanol on metabolic responses to treadmill running in well-trained men. *Journal of Clinical Pharmacology* 33: 136–39.

Kleiner, S.M. 1991. Performance-enhancing aids in sport: health consequences and nutritional alternatives. *Journal of the American College of Nutrition* 10: 163–76.

Krieder, R.B., V. Miriel, and E. Bertun. 1993. Amino acid supplementation and exercise performance: analysis of the proposed ergogenic value. *Sports Medicine* 16: 190–209.

Krieder, R.B., et al. 1996. Effects of ingesting supplements designed to promote lean tissue accretion on body composition during resistance training. *International Journal of Sport Nutrition* 6: 234–46.

Lamb, D.R., et al. 1990. Dietary carbohydrate and intensity of interval swim training. *American Journal of Clinical Nutrition* 52: 1058–63.

Lambert, C.P., et al. 1991. Effects of carbohydrate feeding on multiple-bout resistance exercise. *Journal of Applied Sport Science Research* 5: 192–97.

Lambert, M.I., et al. 1993. Failure of commercial oral amino acid supplements to increase serum growth hormone concentrations in male body-builders. *International Journal of Sport Nutrition* 3: 298–305.

Lefavi, R.G., et al. 1992. Efficacy of chromium supplementation in athletes: emphasis on anabolism. *International Journal of Sport Nutrition* 2: 111–22.

Lemon, P.W.R. 1991. Effect of exercise on protein requirements. *Journal of Sports Sciences* 9: 53–70.

———. 1994. Dietary protein and amino acids. Paper presented at the Nutritional Ergogenic Aids Conference sponsored by the Gatorade Sports Institute, 11–12 November, at Chicago, Illinois.

Manore, M.M., J. Thompson, and M. Russo. 1993. Diet and exercise strategies of a world-class bodybuilder. *International Journal of Sport Nutrition* 3: 76–86.

Manson, J.E., et al. 1994. Vegetable and fruit consumption and incidence of stroke in women. *Circulation* 89: 932.

Maughan, R.J., and D.C. Poole. 1981. The effects of a glycogen-loading regimen on the capacity to perform anaerobic exercise. *European Journal of Applied Physiology* 46: 211–19.

Mazer, E. 1981. Biotin—the little known lifesaver. *Prevention* July: 97–102.

Miller, W.C., M.G. Niederpruem, J.P. Wallace, and A.K. Lindeman. 1994. Dietary fat, sugar, and fiber predict body fat content. *Journal of the American Dietetic Association* 94: 612–15.

National Research Council. 1989. Diet and health: implications for reducing chronic disease risk. Washington, DC: National Academy Press.

Nissen, S., et al. 1996. Effect of leucine metabolite beta-hydroxy-beta-methylbutyrate on muscle metabolism during resistance-exercise training. *Journal of Applied Physiology* 81: 2095–104.

Oakley, G.P., M.J. Adams, and C.M. Dickinson. 1996. More folic acid for everyone, now. *Journal of Nutrition* 126: S751–55.

Olney, J. 1996. Transcript of 60 Minutes, 29 December. CBS, New York.

Scan's Pulse. Editor. 1997. Ergogenic aids: reported facts and claims. Winter Supplement: 15–19.

Seaton, T.B., S.L. Welle, M.K. Warenko, and R.G. Campbell. 1986. Thermic effect of medium and long chain triglycerides in man. *American Journal of Clinical Nutrition* 44: 630–34.

Simko, M.D., and J. Jarosz. 1990. Organic foods: are they better? *Journal of the American Dietetic Association* 90: 367–70.

Sizer F., and E. Whitney. 1994. *Nutrition concepts and controversies*. St. Paul, MN: West.

Slavin, J.L. 1991. Assessing athletes' nutritional status. *The Physician and Sportsmedicine* 19: 79–94.

Somer, E. 1996. Maximum energy: how to eat and exercise for it. *Working Woman*, May, 72–76.

Spiller, G.A., et al. 1987. Effect of protein dose on serum glucose and insulin response to sugars. *American Journal of Clinical Nutrition* 46: 474–80.

Spriet, Larry. Personal communication with author. University of Guelph, Ontario, Canada. Jackman, M., et al. 1994. Caffeine ingestion and high-intensity intermittent exercise. Abstract.

Szlyk, P.C., et al. 1991. Incidence of hypohydration when consuming carbohydrate-electrolyte solutions during field training. *Military Medicine* 156: 399–402.

Tarnopolsky, M.A. 1993. Protein, caffeine, and sports. *The Physician and Sportsmedicine* 21: 137–46.

Thornton, J.S. 1990. How can you tell when an athlete is too thin? *The Physician and Sportsmedicine* 18: 124–33.

Tufts University Diet and Nutrition Letter. 1992. Weak potions for building strong muscles. 10: 7.

Tyler, V.E. 1987. *The new honest herbal: a sensible guide to the use of herbs and related remedies*. Philadelphia: Stickley.

USA Today Magazine. 1995. Most Americans require supplements. October: 8.

U.S. Department of Agriculture and U.S. Department of Health and Human Services. 1995. *Nutrition and your health: dietary guidelines for Americans*. Washington, DC: GPO.

Volek, J.S., et al. 1997. Creatine supplementation enhances muscular performance during high-intensity resistance exercise. *Journal of the American Dietetic Association* 97: 765–70.

Wagner, J.C. 1991. Enhancement of athletic performance with drugs: an overview. *Sports Medicine* 12: 250–65.

Walberg-Rankin, J. 1995. Dietary carbohydrate as an ergogenic aid for prolonged and brief competitions in sport. *International Journal of Sport Nutrition* 5: S13–28.

————. 1994. Ergogenic effects of carbohydrate intake during long- and short-term exercise. Paper presented at Nutritional Ergogenic Aids Conference sponsored by the Gatorade Sports Institute, 11–12 November, at Chicago, Illinois.

Walberg-Rankin, J., et al. 1988. Macronutrient content of a hypoenergy diet affects nitrogen retention and muscle function in weight lifters. *International Journal of Sports Medicine* 9: 261–66.

Walton, R.G., R. Hudak, and R.J. Green-Waite. 1993. Adverse reactions to aspartame: double-blind challenge in patients from a vulnerable population. *Biological Psychiatry* 34: 13–17.

Wardlaw, G.M., P.M. Insel, and M.F. Seyler. 1994. *Contemporary nutrition.* St. Louis: Mosby.

Washington State Department of Agriculture. 1995. Organic food standards. Organic Food Program, Food Safety and Animal Health Division.

Wesson, M., L. McNaughton, P. Davies, and S. Tristram. 1988. Effects of oral administration of aspartic acid salts on the endurance capacity of trained athletes. *Research Quarterly for Exercise and Sport* 59: 234–39.

Wilmore, J.H., and D.L. Costill. 1994. *Physiology of sport and exercise,* 392, 395. Champaign, IL: Human Kinetics.

Winters, L.R., et al. 1992. Riboflavin requirements and exercise adaption in older women. *American Journal of Clinical Nutrition* 56: 526–32.

Zawadzki, K.M., B.B. Yaselkis, and J.L. Ivy. 1992. Carbohydrate-protein complex increases the rate of muscle glycogen storage after exercise. *Journal of Applied Physiology* 72: 1854–59.

INDEX

ABOUT THE AUTHORS

Susan M. Kleiner, PhD, RD, is the foremost authority on eating for strength. In addition to serving as the nutrition consultant to the Cleveland Browns, The Cleveland Cavaliers, and The Repertory Project Dance Company, she's a founding member of the Gatorade Sports Nutrition Speakers Network and a former educational advisory board member of the Gatorade Sports Science Institute. She's also the national spokesperson and scientific expert for the BRITA Company.

Dr. Kleiner is an affiliate assistant professor in the Nutritional Sciences Program at the University of Washington and an adjunct member of the Sarah W. Stedman Center for Nutritional Studies at Duke University Medical Center. The author of *High Performance Nutrition* and a regular columnist and member of the advisory board for both *Shape* and *Men's Fitness*, she has published over 200 articles, chapters, and columns in magazines, scholarly journals, textbooks, and even the *Encyclopaedia Britannica*.

Dr. Kleiner earned her PhD in nutrition at Case Western Reserve University School of Medicine, where she received a Young Investigator Award from the American College of Nutrition for her doctoral research on the cardiovascular disease risks of diet and anabolic steroid use in competitive male bodybuilders. Other awards include the North Carolina Recognized Young Dietitian of the Year and the American Dietetic Association Outstanding Service Award.

Dr. Kleiner is a fellow of the American College of Nutrition and a member of the American College of Sports Medicine, the American Dietetic Association, and its Sports, Cardiovascular and Wellness Nutritionists Practice Group.

She lives in Mercer Island, Washington, with her husband Jeffrey and two daughters. She enjoys strength training, hiking, swimming, creative cooking, and music.

Maggie Greenwood-Robinson is the author of *21 Days to Better Fitness* and the coauthor of eight other fitness books. Her articles have appeared in *Women's Sports and Fitness*, *Working Woman*, *MuscleMag International*, *Ironman*, *Muscle and Fitness*, *Female Bodybuilding*, and many other publications. She has conducted seminars on strength training, exercise motivation, diet and nutrition, fat loss, and couple's fitness, and she has taught bodyshaping classes at the University of Southern Indiana. Maggie is a certified nutrition consultant.

She and her husband Jeffry live in Newburgh, Indiana, where she enjoys strength training, low-fat cooking, and Bible study.